The Agonist

Volume X, Issue II, Spring 2017

Nietzsche & Epicureanism

Keith Ansell-Pearson

Daniel Conway   Matthew Dennis   Jennifer O. Gammage

Peter S. Groff   Jean-Marie Guyau   Jill Marsden

Joseph M. Spencer   Federico Testa   Willow Verkerk

Contents

Book Reviews

Editors' Introduction

We are excited to be hosting Dr. Keith Ansell-Pearson who serves as the Guest Editor for this issue on Nietzsche and Epicureanism. Nietzsche's relationship to Epicurus, and to all other post-Socratic schools, still remains to be explored in the unchartered territories of philosophy as a way of life. Six essays examine this relationship from different angles. We are thankful to Federico Testa for translating the piece by Jean-Marie Guyau for *The Agonist*. We would like to thank Dr. Ansell-Pearson for putting this issue together and all the other contributors, Dr. Daniel Conway, Dr. Peter S. Groff, Dr. Jill Marsden, Dr. Verkerk, Matthew Denis, and Federico Testa. We extend our gratitude to our reviewers, Jennifer Gammage and Dr. Joseph M. Spencer.

In the last several months, since October 2016, Nietzsche Circle has co-organized events with The National Psychological Association for Psychoanalysis (based in New York City) to explore not only Nietzsche's connection to psychoanalysis, but also the relationship between philosophy and psychoanalysis in general. In these events we heard many interesting talks and plan to create an issue on this topic, and we will open it to a wider range of researchers and practitioners through a call for papers. Those practitioners who do research in this area, please contact us.

We welcome Alec Ontiveros on board who joined the Circle recently. Alec will oversee the electronic publication of the journal. We look forward to working with him. We also look forward to hearing from our readers with their ideas on new subjects to explore or if they are willing to write reviews for us.

The Editorial Board
March 2017

Guest Editor's Introduction

Keith Ansell-Pearson

      With a few notable exceptions the extent to which Nietzsche sought in his writings to revitalize the teaching of Epicurus has been overlooked in the literature on him. Epicurus was important to Nietzsche on account of the nature of his philosophical *practice* – "heroic-idyllic" – and the fact that this practice involved philosophy as a mode of life, an art of existing, and a unique way of being in the world. Nietzsche was keen in his lifetime to create and cultivate his own Epicurean garden. As he puts it in a letter to his amanuensis Peter Gast, dated March 26, 1879: "Where do we want to renew the Garden of Epicurus?" (KSB 5, 399)

      Although Nietzsche claimed to have experienced the character of Epicurus differently, to everybody else he was not alone in the nineteenth century in employing the name of "Epicurus" to signal the need for a reformation of philosophy in accordance with Epicurean principles of living. For Marx, writing in the 1840s, and in defiance of Hegel's negative assessment, Epicurus is the "greatest representative of the Greek enlightenment,"[1] whilst for Jean-Marie Guyau, writing in the 1870s, Epicurus is the original free spirit, "Still today it is the spirit of old Epicurus who, combined with new doctrines, works away at and undermines Christianity."[2] For Nietzsche, Epicurus is one of the greatest human beings to have graced the earth and the inventor of "heroic-idyllic philosophizing" (WS 295). Nietzsche's interest in Epicurus, which is most prominent in these writings, is, on the face of it, curious: what interest does he have in a philosopher of antiquity who was an egalitarian, offered what Cicero called a "plebeian" philosophy, and who espoused a simple-minded hedonic theory of value? These are all positions we would expect Nietzsche to have no truck with. And yet, especially in the middle period, he is full of praise for the figure of Epicurus. This set of specially commissioned essays seeks to explore Nietzsche's interest in Epicurus in fresh and innovative ways.

---

[1] Marx, Karl. 'Difference Between the Democritean and Epicurean Philosophy of Nature', 73.

[2] Guyau, Jean-Marie. *La Morale D'Epicure* , 280.

Like the other nineteenth century interpreters I have referred to, Nietzsche is acutely aware that Epicurean doctrine has been greatly maligned and misunderstood in the history of thought. One commentator on Epicurus's philosophy speaks of the "slanders and fallacies of a long and unfriendly tradition" and invites us to reflect on Epicurus as at one and the same time the most revered and most reviled of all founders of philosophy in the Greco-Roman world.[3] Since the time of the negative assessment by Cicero and the early Church Fathers, "Epicureanism has been used as a smear word – a rather general label indicating atheism, selfishness, and debauchery."[4] As Nietzsche observes in *The Wanderer and His Shadow:*

> Epicurus has been alive in all ages and lives now, unknown to those who have called and call themselves Epicureans, and enjoying no reputation among philosophers. He has, moreover, himself forgotten his own name: it was the heaviest burden he ever cast off (WS 227).

Two aphorisms from *Assorted Opinions and Maxims* reveal the importance Epicurus holds for Nietzsche in his middle period. In the first Nietzsche confesses to having dwelled like Odysseus in the underworld and says that he will often be found there again. As someone who sacrifices so as to talk to the dead, he states that there are four pairs of thinkers from whom he will accept judgement, and Epicurus and Montaigne make up the first pair he mentions (AOM 408).[5] In the second aphorism Epicurus, along with the Stoic Epictetus, is revered as a thinker in whom wisdom assumes bodily form (AOM 224). The point is perhaps obvious: philosophy is not simply sophistry or mere *paideia* but an incorporated practice that enables the individual to negotiate and affirm the most demanding and challenging questions of existence, including, notably, such tests of the self as the fact of our mortality and the question of how to live.

In what follows the contributors to the special issue of *The Agonist* undertake a fresh exploration of Nietzsche's appreciation of Epicurus and of the Epicurean motifs that characterize his writings. In her essay Jill Marsden asks how Nietzsche "experiences the character" of Epicurus. It is argued that Nietzsche "discovers" Epicurus on his thought paths during the middle period of his writings and that

---

[3] De Witt, Norman Wentworth. *Epicurus and His Philosophy,* 3

[4] Leddy, Neven & Lifschitz Avi S. (eds.), *Epicurus in the Enlightenment,* 4.

[5] The other three pairs are: Goethe and Spinoza, Plato and Rousseau, and Pascal and Schopenhauer. On Montaigne's relation to Epicurean doctrine see Howard Jones, *Nietzsche and the Epicurean Tradition* (London and New York: Routledge, 1992), 159-62.

his very physical way of philosophizing develops in proximity to Epicurus as part of a thinking relationship with the earth. Taking the "happiness of the afternoon of antiquity" (GS 45) as a clue, it is suggested that Epicurus is a surprising source for Nietzsche's experience of *amor fati* as the affective precondition for eternal return.

Next Willow Verkerk explores how Nietzsche's joyful friendship, active especially in the free spirit texts of the middle period, shares with Epicurus an emphasis on health, community, and freedom from the fear of death. Nietzsche wants to renew the Epicurean garden by creating a community of free spirits who will experience pleasure through shared reflection and self-affirmation. In *The Gay Science* (aphorism 338) Nietzsche emphasizes that friends should share joy not suffering and in *Human All Too Human* he writes that "Fellow rejoicing (*Mitfreude*), not fellow suffering (*Mitleiden*) makes the friend" (HAH 499). After examining how Epicurus' writings on community and health are reflected in Nietzsche's middle period, this essay focuses on the therapeutic role of Nietzsche's joyful friendship. She argues that the joyful friendship is most praised by Nietzsche for its capacity to become a healing balm for the wounds of pity (*Mitleid*), which represent our more fundamental feeling of the fear of death. In Nietzsche's joyful friendship, the friends turn away from the burden of mortality and, in an Epicurean fashion, turn to the *lived* activities of the everyday to heal the self.

In his contribution Keith Ansell-Pearson seeks to illuminate some fundamental aspects of Nietzsche's search for happiness and joy. As Richard Bett has noted, Nietzsche likes to give the impression that he is against happiness altogether.[6] A well-known aphorism in a late text, *Twilight of the Idols*, is typical in this regard: "Humanity does not strive for happiness; only the English do that" (TI "Maxims and Arrows," 12). However, an examination of Nietzsche, especially of the neglected middle period texts, can show that he is deeply concerned with the fate of happiness and also that he develops rich conceptions of pleasure and joy. Ansell-Pearson explores various renditions of happiness and joy in Nietzsche's writings, offering a series of perspectives on the topic. He focuses on some key aphorisms – GS 45 and WS 295 – in which Nietzsche celebrates Epicurus for his modest but voluptuous appreciation of existence and for inventing the practice of "heroic-idyllic philosophizing."

Peter S. Groff examines Nietzsche's conflicted relation to Epicurus. He focuses in particular on the Epicurean credo "live unnoticed" (*lathe biōsas*), which

---

[6] Bett, Richard 'Nietzsche, the Greeks, and Happiness' 45—70, 45.

advocated an inconspicuous life of quiet philosophical reflection, self-cultivation and friendship, avoiding the public radar and eschewing the larger ambitions and perturbations of political life, and track its influence on Nietzsche's thought and life. Perhaps unsurprisingly, the idea looms largest and is most warmly received in Nietzsche's middle period writings, where one finds a repeated concern with prudence, withdrawal and concealment, and where the primary emphasis is on private pluralistic experiments in therapeutic self-cultivation among small groups of free spirits. The idea of the Epicurean Garden appeals greatly to Nietzsche at this time. However, Nietzsche's growing impatience with human imperfections and the siren song of great politics (*grosse Politik*) eventually lead him away from Epicurus and to Plato. The more ambitious philosopher-legislator who takes upon himself the task of determining the future of humanity now replaces the paradigm of the modest, hidden helpful philosopher-therapist. Nonetheless, Groff argues that we can profit more from the modest, practical insights of Nietzsche's Epicurean art of living.

In his contribution Daniel Conway's aim is to document the Epicurean themes that Nietzsche imports into *Ecce Homo* (1888). Intent on presenting himself as having surpassed Epicurus as a teacher and healer, Nietzsche acknowledges his own share in the *décadence* that grips late modern European culture, only to assert nonetheless that he remains a destiny. According to his own presentation of himself and his newly consecrated way of life, Nietzsche is poised to succeed precisely where Epicurus failed—namely, in providing an exemplified way of life that caters to those who are healthy, those who reasonably may hope to convalescence, and those who may actively "oppose" the *décadence* imprinted on them by the late modern epoch.

In their contribution Federico Testa and Matthew Dennis explore a comparison between Jean-Marie Guyau (1854-88) and Nietzsche centred on the importance and place of Epicurus and Epicureanism in their works. In order to contribute to the development of this intersection between the two authors through the shared reference to Hellenistic tradition, they also present a translation of Guyau's 'Introduction' to his book *La Morale d'Épicure* from 1878. In the introductory essay which precedes the translation, they show how both the young Guyau and Nietzsche in his middle period writings are inspired by Epicurean philosophy, especially in their commitment to an ethics of pleasure and pleasurable living. Both Nietzsche and Guyau stress the importance of the Hellenistic model of self-cultivation, consisting of the active and rational processes of shaping one's life through philosophical practice. The Epicurean sage is for the young Guyau an "artist of existence"; similarly Nietzsche finds in Epicurus a master of self-cultivation through "modest voluptuousness."

Although it can only be speculated whether he read Guyau's monograph on Epicurus, Nietzsche's annotations to other texts of Guyau's, such as his *A Sketch of Morality Independent of Obligation of Sanction*, reveal an enthusiastic reading of Guyau, which is perhaps unsurprising given the many congruencies in theme and method that each philosopher shares.

It is to be hoped that this set of essays serves to inspire future research into Nietzsche's relation to Hellenistic philosophy, especially Epicurus and Epicureanism, and into the re-invention of philosophy as a way of life in the modern period. In conclusion let me indicate why I think a focus on Nietzsche's Epicureanism is so important for research and our thinking today.

In recent writings I have contended that an ethos of Epicurean enlightenment pervades Nietzsche's middle writings with Epicurus celebrated for his teachings on mortality and the cultivation of modest pleasures. Although the late Nietzsche has some problems with Epicurus, in his middle writings he writes in praise of him and draws upon his philosophy as a way of promoting what we can call an Epicurean care of self and world. We need to discover this Nietzsche for ourselves and in part as a way of contesting Martin Heidegger's reading of Nietzsche that focuses on the late writings, mostly the *Nachlass*, and construes all the major concepts of the late period, notably the will to power and the overman, as indicating that Nietzsche is the "technological" thinker of our age and whose major concept is the will to power and its desire for mastery of the earth though the will to will. My view is that we need a much more subtle and nuanced appreciation of Nietzsche than the Heideggerian reading permits, and one way to develop this is to focus on the neglected middle writings and especially the reception of Epicurus.

Within so-called continental philosophy Heidegger's "Nietzsche" has perhaps been the dominant influence. It has at least two main contentions: first, that the real Nietzsche is to be found in the *Nachlass* of the mid to late 1880s, and second that Nietzsche does not overcome metaphysics, as he claims to do, but merely inverts it. [7] For all the impressive brilliance of his reading, Heidegger's

---

[7] On the one hand, Heidegger contends that Nietzsche finds himself as a thinker in the years between 1880 and 1883 – but this period covers core texts, such as *Dawn*, that he never subjects to analysis and about which he has nothing to say (with the exception of some remarks about, and analysis of, *The Gay Science*). On the other hand, he maintains that, "Nietzsche's philosophy proper…did not assume a final form and was not published in any book, neither in the decade between 1879 and 1889 nor during the years preceding. What Nietzsche himself published during his creative life was always foreground". M. Heidegger, *Nietzsche. Volume One. The Will to Power as Art*, trans. David Farrell Krell (London: Routledge and Kegan Paul, 1981), 8-9.

confrontation with Nietzsche carries real dangers: the thesis that Nietzsche is the last metaphysician of the West has arguably led to sterility in continental receptions of Nietzsche and, more pressingly perhaps, we lose sight of the practical-therapeutic dimension of Nietzsche's philosophy and its attempt to overcome metaphysics; and we stop reading the published texts. In my view the costs have been high and it is now time to focus our attention on the published texts and the actual and, in many instances, neglected details of Nietzsche's search for philosophy.

Let me list what I see as some of Nietzsche's principal concerns in his middle period writings and that serve to inspire him to pursue an Epicurean path:

- A critique of commercial society and an emerging consumer culture.
- A commitment to stable pleasures and mental equilibrium over the need for perpetual change.
- An attempt to live free of the delusions of human exceptionalism, and free from the gods, especially the fear of the gods.
- An emphasis on a therapy of slowness and the *vita contemplativa*, including a tempering of the human mind in order to liberate it from moral and religious fanaticism.
- The search for a simpler existence purified of the metaphysical need with an attention to the importance of the closest things.
- A care of self that is intended to be coextensive with the whole of life, suggesting an ecological rather than atomistic approach to the art of living.
- The need to conquer unjustified fears and to reinstitute the role played by chance and chance events in the world and in human existence.
- In contrast to a teaching on the salvation of the soul Nietzsche favours one that attends to the needs of the body and that takes the body as its starting-point. A neglect of the body, for example, through a teaching of pure spirituality, leads one to self-hatred and produces melancholic individuals.

In his middle period, then, Epicurus is one of Nietzsche's chief inspirations in his effort to liberate himself from the metaphysical need and to aid humanity in its need to now cure its neuroses. It could be argued that this endeavour – to heal the earth and cultivate a new human relation to it – remains a pertinent one today: we live in a world facing ecological catastrophe and driven by anthropocentric pollution. The task of an Epicurean enlightenment, of the kind Nietzsche undertakes in his middle period writings, has never been more pressing or urgent.

Works Cited

Bett, Richard. 'Nietzsche, the Greeks, and Happiness (with special reference to Aristotle and Epicurus),' *Philosophical Topics*, 33: 2, 2005, 45—70, 45.

De Witt, Norman Wentworth. *Epicurus and His Philosophy* (Minneapolis: University of Minnesota Press, 1954).

Guyau, Jean-Marie. *La Morale D'Epicure* (Paris: Librairie Gemer Baillière, 1878). Leddy, Neven & Lifschitz Avi S. (eds.), *Epicurus in the Enlightenment* (Oxford: Voltaire Foundation, 2009).

Marx, Karl. 'Difference Between the Democritean and Epicurean Philosophy of Nature' in K.

Marx & F. Engels, *Collected Works: Volume One 1835-43* (London: Lawrence & Wishart, 1975).

.

Essays

In Proximity to Epicurus:
Nietzsche's Discovery of the Past Within

Jill Marsden

We need history, for the past continues to flow within us in a hundred waves; we ourselves are, indeed, nothing but that which at every moment we sense of this continued flowing [...]The last three centuries very probably still continue to live on, in all their cultural colours and cultural refractions, *close beside us*: they want only to be *discovered*. (AOM, 223)[1]

A few short millennia before the ocean of impersonal forces arrayed a small assortment of its parts into a man called Friedrich Nietzsche, it spent a little time disporting itself before the senses of Epicurus. It presented itself in the guise of the sea, and sky, and clouds, and mineral formations, as animals large and small, as ideas, as feelings, as specific kinds of thoughts and mood. Later when these impersonal forces folded some tiny part of themselves into Nietzsche, something of their past presence in Epicurus's world stirred within his own:

> Epicurus. - Yes, I am proud of the fact that I experience [empfinden] the character of Epicurus differently to perhaps anyone else, and enjoy in all that I read and hear of him the happiness of the afternoon of antiquity: - I see his eye gazing out on a vast, white sea, over the rocks along the shoreline where the sun lies, whilst big and small animals play in its light, secure and serene like this light and that eye itself. Such happiness could only have been invented by one who is suffering continually, the happiness of an eye looking out on a becalmed sea of existence and which can now no longer tire of its surface, and the colourful, tender, quivering skin of the sea. Never before has sensuality been so modest. (GS 45)

Contemplating the delicate shuddering waves, Epicurus enjoys a serene happiness, which across the centuries will lap at the shore of a Genovese coast on another restful summer day (KSA 8/527/30[31]). "Experiencing the character" of the ancient Greek philosopher from Samos, Nietzsche writes from

---

[1] Translations are my own.

the Italian Riviera in 1881 as one who inhabits the atmosphere of the afternoon of antiquity, his physiology attuned to the constellation of affects named "Epicurus". "Den Charakter Epikur's anders .. empfinden" involves a physical encounter with "temperament" or "nature" (Charakter), "empfinden" meaning "to sense", "perceive", "feel". In channelling these forces, Nietzsche feels an affinity of disposition, something more fundamental than intellectual empathy or philosophical debt. It is as if the ancient philosopher "lives on" in his thinking, confirming the declaration that he makes in the aphorism "*The eternal Epicurus*": "Epicurus has lived at all times and is living still, unbeknown to those who have called and call themselves Epicurean, and without reputation amongst philosophers" (WS 227). When Nietzsche claims to experience the character of Epicurus differently to others, he may intend the point atavistically, as the awareness within himself of sensibilities from the past. [2]

In what follows, I explore what it might mean for Nietzsche to experience the character[3] of Epicurus and to "feel" powers of the past "within himself" (GS 10). A starting point will be to ask why he should envisage Epicurus by the shore, resting his eye upon the "sea of existence". It is notable that another well-known passage in praise of Epicurus, "Et in Arcadia ego" (*The Wanderer and his Shadow*, 295), also evokes a particular landscape, atmosphere and time of day, here a sun-lit valley around half past five. Both pieces of writing concern the feeling of joy occasioned by the vividly detailed scene and both describe panoramas very familiar to Nietzsche from his European travels. Whilst these passages do not appear to contribute much to the scholarly task of evaluating Nietzsche's relation to Epicurus, their focus on the climate and landscape of experience is instructive. It will be suggested that Nietzsche's practice of philosophy develops in proximity to Epicurus in a very physical sense as part of a thinking relationship with the earth. Taking the "happiness of the afternoon of antiquity" as a clue, I trace a "thought path" that links Epicurus to the experience of *amor fati* as the affective precondition for Nietzsche's eternal return.

*

---

[2] In *The Gay Science* Nietzsche suggests that although these archaic powers may seem strange, rare and extraordinary in the present day, they may once have been common. Accordingly, it behoves whoever "feels these powers in oneself" to care for, defend, honour and cultivate them "against another world that resists them" (GS 10).

[3] This is somewhat different to the act of 'identifying' with Epicurus. For a discussion of Epicurus as a model Nietzsche uses in 'in the process of creating himself' see Wilson H. Shearin 2014, p.74.

That Nietzsche was preoccupied with the optimum climate and landscape for his thought is amply demonstrated by his private notes, letters and autobiographical reflections in addition to the copious references in his published works. Two texts from Nietzsche's "middle period", *Dawn* (1881) and *The Gay Science* (1882), were produced during his time on the Italian Riviera (the Liguria region). In *Ecce Homo* Nietzsche likens both the text of *Dawn* and its author to a basking sea beast, sunbathing amongst the rocks near to Genoa where "almost every sentence of that book was thought, *hatched* [*erschlüpft*]" (EH "Books", D, 1). Alone and sharing 'secrets with the sea" (EH "Books", D, 1), the thinker's ideas incubate in the warmth, abundant sentences unfold in the sun. In praise of this work site Nietzsche writes to Franz Overbeck:

> I think so often about you, especially in the afternoon when almost every day I sit or lie in my secluded cliffs along the coast, resting like a lizard in the sun, while my thoughts embark on some adventure of the spirit. My diet and the division of the day should eventually do me good! Sea air and clear skies: now I see that these are indispensable to me! (KSB,6,57).

Nietzsche writes to Peter Gast and to his mother and his sister on the same day, repeating the lizard image and enthusing about the beneficial effects of the sea and clear sky on his health (KSB, 6, 56-57). As is immediately apparent from these remarks, Nietzsche's description of himself sequestered among the rocks in the afternoon sun calls to mind his representation of Epicurus. Writing to friends about this Genovese coast he likens its solitude to that of "an island of the Greek archipelago" (KSB, 7, 259); "no doubt about it, there is something *Greek* about this place" (KSB, 7, 261). In such a setting it is possible that lines of Epicurean verse lap at the edge of his consciousness, as he takes pleasure in watching the sea.[4] It is also worth noting that in this letter to Overbeck the blessings of the climate (sea air and clear skies) are married with more domestic matters (diet, division of the day) to form the indispensable requirements for the thinker. As this letter and many similar ones indicate, philosophy for Nietzsche is shaped by the vital forces of the body and its environment and, reciprocally, thought belongs to particular locations and climatic conditions. In *Dawn*, Nietzsche suggests that his philosophy might be seen as a "translation" into reason of the "circuitous paths" of his drives: drives for "gentle sunlight, bright and buoyant air, southerly vegetation, the breath of the sea, fleeting meals of meat, eggs and fruit .." (D 553). To "embark on some adventure of the spirit" – as Nietzsche reports doing in his

---

[4] See Book II of Lucretius's *De Rerum Natura* (Gaskin 1995, p. 120).

secluded cliffs along the coast – it is necessary to attend to an array of "worldly" things.

Such material concerns are constant features on Nietzsche's horizon. In correspondence to Overbeck from St. Moritz, Nietzsche likens his fastidious attention to small details to a classical style of living:

> The air is almost better than Sorrento, and is full of fragrances, the way I like it. The way I divide my day, my life-style, my diet – these things would not have dishonoured a wise man of old: everything *very simple* and yet a system of fifty sometimes very delicate considerations. (KSB, 5, 425)

As is well known, Epicurus commends the wisdom of the simple life and liberation from unwholesome desires.[5] Keith Ansell Pearson proposes that "Nietzsche is attracted to the Epicurean emphasis on the modesty of a human existence", exemplified by simple pleasures and philosophising in a garden, away from public view (Ansell Pearson 2014, 3): "A small garden, figs, little cheeses and in addition, three or four good friends – that was the opulence of Epicurus" (WS 192). In his letters to Peter Gast during the 1880s, Nietzsche makes frequent reference to the idea of Epicurus's garden, reflecting repeatedly on the environment in which Epicurus thinks: "*Where* are we going to revive the garden of Epicurus?" (KSB, 5, 399); "What I envy in Epicurus are the disciples in his garden.." (KSB, 6, 436). He even compliments Gast for "everything redolent of the air and fragrance of Epicurus's garden" that has emanated from his recent letters (KSB, 6, 428-9).

The importance of these physical conditions and parochial concerns is formulated most explicitly in *The Wanderer and his Shadow*, where Nietzsche claims that the discipline of philosophy has been wrongly orientated towards the "farthest things" such as metaphysical questions of immortality, god and the soul (WS 6). By contrast, the most immediate "nearest things" [*nächste Dinge*] such as the division of the day, eating, sleeping and other "small and everyday" matters have been poorly regarded, a fact which Nietzsche claims accounts for "*almost all the physical and psychical frailties* of the individual" (WS 6). Undoubtedly this failing stems from the Platonic-Christian legacy that the "nearest" and "farthest things" are fundamentally different in kind, the latter having been prized as idealities, ungrounded in matter and removed from active processes of materialization ("culture"). Because these realms have been regarded as mutually discontinuous, the world is perceived as a mass of isolated beings, unitary souls and brute material

---

[5] See "Letter to Menoeceus" (Gaskin 1995, p.45).

forms. However, for Nietzsche, the "nearest things" embrace "systems" rather than entities ("health", "upbringing", "nature"), [6] and share with Epicurean thinking idiosyncrasies such as "retreat from politics" and "use of moods and atmospheric conditions".[7] The overarching factor uniting the two philosophers is their faith in the wisdom of the earth, their sensitivity to matters that are "close".

The "nearest things" include personal preferences and some eccentric proclivities, but attention to these things is not about knowing "who" you are; it is about knowing the formative forces that progressively "make" you. For example, in *Ecce Homo*, Nietzsche identifies the impact of the nearest things in terms of the task of "becoming what one is": "little things" like nutriment, place, climate and recreation "are more important than anything that has been considered of importance hitherto" (EH, 'Clever', 10). However, lest this seem a simple determinism it is essential to recognise that the physical environment in which writing and thought are possible is reciprocally conditioned by prevailing beliefs. Material forces influence thought but ideas also have physical effects on the body. Nietzsche integrates this idea into a draft for section 341 of *The Gay Science* in which the thought of the eternal return is first announced. To the anticipated question "But if everything is necessary, how can I be in charge of my own actions?" (KSA/9/11[143]) Nietzsche gives the following response: "You say that food, place, air, society shape and determine you? Well, your concepts do still more for these determine you to this food, place, air, society" (KSA/9/11[143]). The fundamental point is that if you "incorporate" (einverleiben) the "thought of thoughts" it will *physically change you* (9/11[143]). Such an outlandish proposition is unthinkable within the Platonic-Christian worldview which can only understand matter by recourse to the powers of a 'higher' realm. Things may be otherwise for Nietzsche's Epicurus, his eye never straying beyond the horizon. Alert to the turbulent depths of existence, he never tires of contemplating the surface of 'this world'.

---

[6] Nietzsche lists his "Doctrine of the Nearest Things" in his private notes as follows: "*Division* of the day, purpose of the day (periods). Nourishment. Company [Umgang]. Nature. Solitude. Sleep. Profession [Broderwerb]. Upbringing (original and foreign). Use of moods and atmospheric conditions (*Witterung*). Health. Retreat from politics."See KSA 8/581/40[16].

[7] See Nietzsche's list at KSA 8/581/40[16]. Various sayings attributed to Epicurus concern a retreat from public office and political life. For example, "We must release ourselves from the prison of affairs and politics" ("Vatican Sayings", LVIII, cited in Gaskin p. 52). See also Gaskin 64, 71. Epicurus's remarks on meterological phenomena are to be found in his "Letter to Pythocles" (see Gaskin 1995, pp. 30-41).

According to Keith Ansell Pearson, it is "from Epicurus that Nietzsche gets the inspiration to give up on what he calls the first and last things, the questions of a theologically inspired metaphysics, and devote attention to the closest things" (Ansell Pearson 2013, 104). This view is supported by the fact that the two sections of *The Wanderer and his Shadow* (WS 5 & 6) which introduce the doctrine of the nearest things are directly succeeded by a lengthy passage on the consolations of Epicurean teaching. The "wonderful insight" which Nietzsche attributes to Epicurus is the realisation that to quell the tempests of the soul "it is absolutely not necessary to have resolved the ultimate and outermost theoretical questions" (WS 7). Faith in the notion of ultimate truth is undermined by Epicurus's embrace of a "multiplicity of hypotheses" and by his insistence on the gods' disregard for the affairs of mortals (WS 7). The proximity of Epicurus is also felt in the closing section of *The Wanderer and the Shadow*:

> Only to *the enobled man will the freedom of spirit* be granted; to him alone does the *alleviation of life* approach and salve his wounds; he first must say that he lives for *joy* and for the sake of no further goal; and in any other mouth his motto would be dangerous: *Peace around me and goodwill to all nearest things*. (WS 350)

To live for joy and for the sake of no other goal is to make a profound affirmation. The state of serene calmness (*ataraxia*) so highly valued by Epicurus is achieved through a grateful embrace of life and particularly an embrace of the nearest things, the gifts of the earth.

Book Four of *The Gay Science* opens with an affirmation made for the New Year: "*Amor fati*: let that be my love from now on!" (GS 276). Vowing to love fate, Nietzsche speaks about wanting only to be a "Yes-Sayer" and not an "accuser" (GS 276). Again, the proximity of Epicurus is felt in Nietzsche's writings for this section is directly followed by a passage entitled "Personal providence" which affirms the beauty of chance and commends the "gods of Epicurus" to the extent that these "carefree and unknown ones" have no involvement with the petty concerns of mortals (GS 277). In *Philosophy as a Way of Life*, Pierre Hadot alludes to E. Hoffman's claim that "it is precisely because the Epicurean considered existence to be the result of pure chance that he greeted each moment with immense gratitude, like a kind of divine miracle" (Hadot, 252). Indeed, to feel good will to all nearest things is to mark a decisive break with the forces which "accuse life" and to affirm a this-worldly love of the here and now. This bears on the relation of thought to its "physical" context because Epicurean philosophy cannot thrive with the big cities which lack quiet and expansive places for reflection and which are dominated by ostentatious monuments to 'otherworldly' discourse (GS 280). In "Architecture for those who wish to pursue knowledge", Nietzsche writes that the abandoned churches will not meet the needs of the secular thinker: "we godless ones could not think *our thoughts* in such surroundings" (GS 280). The environment for god-less philosophy must be conducive to its this-worldly flourishing: "We want to see *ourselves* translated into stone and plants, we want to take walks *in ourselves* when we wander around these buildings and gardens" (GS 280).

To see ourselves translated into stones and plants, to take circuitous paths "in ourselves" as we stroll around buildings and gardens is to refuse the basic Platonic-Christian presumption of the "inner" sanctum of thought. In section 291 of *The Gay Science* entitled "Genoa", Nietzsche says that he has studied the buildings and landscapes of this city for a long time and declares that he can see the "faces" of past generations.

> Genoa. – I have looked upon this city for a good while, its villas and pleasure gardens and the wide circuits of its inhabited heights and slopes. Finally I must say this: I see *faces* of past generations. This district is strewn with the images of bold and autocratic men. They have *lived* and have wanted to live on - they say so with their houses, built and decorated for centuries, and not for the fleeting hour: they were well disposed to life [sie waren dem Leben gut], however ill-disposed they may often have been towards themselves. (GS 291)

To become well-disposed to life manifests itself as a desire to live on. This is not a desire for immortality but for the externalization of desire, its manifestation in things. For Nietzsche, thought is in the world, not in the thinker. All the default settings of language militate against travelling with this idea. To think of the soul or self as an internal entity is a Christian prejudice. For Nietzsche, souls are not unitary, immaterial, ghosts of another world. On the contrary, rare human beings of an age are best thought of as "the suddenly emerging after-shoots [*plötzlich auftauchende Nachschösslinge*] of past cultures and their powers: as atavisms of a people and its ethos" (GS 10). In a wonderful passage, "Why we have to travel" (AOM 223) Nietzsche claims that "the past continues to flow within us in a hundred waves; we ourselves are, indeed, nothing but that which at every moment we sense of this continued flowing" (AOM 223). The traveller soon discovers that one cannot step into the river of one's most intimate being twice. Moreover, the one who becomes adept in the "subtler art of travel" will rediscover the adventurous migrations of his ego "in the process of becoming and transformation" in many countries and ages, in Egypt and Greece, Byzantium and Rome, "in the Renaissance and the Reformation, at home and abroad, indeed in the sea, the forests, in the plants and in the mountains" (AOM 223). One rediscovers the flows of the past in oneself with every fresh encounter, finding within *this world* hitherto unguessed at depths.

Directly after this passage in *Assorted Opinions and Maxims*, Nietzsche speaks of ages in which the senses are so blocked that they are incapable of hearing the voice of reason and philosophy or of seeing "wisdom that wanders in bodily form [die leibhaft wandelnde Weisheit] whether it bears the name of Epictetus or of Epicurus" [AOM 224]. "Wisdom walking in bodily form" implies a thinking relationship with the material environment, an alertness to the sensory richness of air, temperature, fragrance and light. Like Epicurus, who embodies this wisdom, Nietzsche traces thought-paths which meander through the landscape, through buildings and gardens, translating themselves into stones and plants. Whatever is read or heard by Nietzsche is carried into the open where it quickly sloughs off its scholarly scent. His habit is to "think outdoors [im Freien zu denken], walking, jumping, climbing, dancing, preferably on lonely mountains or close by the sea where even the paths become thoughtful" (GS 366). In this way, thoughts belong to a particular atmosphere, to a time and place of their genesis. It is a rationalist prejudice to separate ideas from their conditions as if their blossoming was independent of all nutrients. When Nietzsche declares that paths become "thoughtful", this is not a metaphor for an intellectual journey but a description of how thinking is part of a climate and a landscape. A provisional title for *The Wanderer and his Shadow* was "Thought-paths of St Moritz" (KSA 8, 610). Almost all of it was written in six pocket-sized notebooks that Nietzsche carried with him on hikes through the hills and around the lakes of St. Moritz, Silvaplana and Sils Maria.[8] Among the few notes gathered under this title, Nietzsche describes a sublime experience of "heroic-idyllic" power.

> The day before yesterday, towards evening, I was completely immersed in Claude Lorrainian raptures and finally burst into lengthy, intense crying. That I was still to experience this! I had not known that the earth could display this and had believed that good painters had invented it. The heroic-idyllic is now the discovery of my soul; and everything bucolic of the ancients has become all at once unveiled to me and made manifest – until now I did not understand anything of this. (KSA 8, 610, 43[3])

Nietzsche's discovery of the "heroic-idyllic" in St Moritz is an encounter with ancient forces "living on" *close beside him*. This profound experience is the

---

[8] See Krell and Bates 1997, pp.123-123.

inspiration for a striking passage in *The Wanderer and his Shadow* entitled "Et in Arcadia ego" (WS 295), in which Nietzsche describes stumbling upon an uncannily mythic landscape. The ground is vivid with flowers and grasses, "waves of hills" cascade to a "milky green lake". Overwhelmed with the beauty of the place, he trembles in wordless adoration of "the moment [*Augenblick*] of its revelation":

> Unconsciously, as if it were only natural, one transposed Hellenic heroes into this pure, clear world of light (which had nothing about it of yearning or expectancy, no looking forward or backward); one had to feel it as Poussin and his pupil would have done — at once heroic and idyllic. And so too have individual people *lived*, and have constantly *felt* themselves to be in the world and the world in them and among them one of the greatest men, the inventor of a heroic-idyllic form of philosophy: Epicurus. (WS 295)

Epicurus is 'experienced' on Nietzsche's thought path in the midst of the Swiss mountains. Charged with ancient sensibilities, the traveller conjures Hellenic spirits from a newly enchanted earth. Without forethought Greek heroes are summoned forth, with no trace of yearning or expectancy, no "looking forward or backward". To live without desire or expectation, without longing for the future or lingering in the past, is to live in the eternity of the moment. In St Moritz, Nietzsche realises that this is how individuals have actually lived; more, this is how "they have enduringly *felt* they existed in the world and the world existed in them" (WS, 295). When Epicurean affects are transmitted is this entrancing "clear world of light," heroic idyllic philosophy is lived and felt as a profound affirmation of the earth. The character of Epicurus, one "of the greatest men," is experienced by Nietzsche as overwhelming love of fate: "My formula for greatness in a human being is *amor fati* .. that one wants nothing to be other than it is, not forwards not backwards, not in all eternity." (EH, "Clever", 10).

Love of fate is only possible when one feels oneself to be part of the world. To live without *ressentiment*, to love the things of the earth, is to achieve a state of Epicurean tranquillity. On the untitled page that lies between the foreword and the first section of *Ecce Homo*, Nietzsche expresses a supreme gratitude to his "whole life".[9] The image is a rich and fertile one, a perfect moment of sun-lit brilliance:

---

[9] Richard Bett notes that Pierre Hadot includes Nietzsche in his discussion of the value of the present instant in ancient philosophy, citing a passage on saying yes to eternity by saying yes to a single moment. However, he does not see any relevant link to Epicurus:

On this perfect day, when everything has become ripe and not only the grapes are growing brown, a ray of sunlight has fallen on to my life: I looked behind me, I looked before me, never have I seen so many and such good things together.

This 'goodwill to all nearest things' is an expression of gratitude for the bounty of the earth. To become 'so well disposed' to life that you would fervently desire its eternal return it is necessary to make an affirmative pact with fate. As Joseph P. Vincenzo writes, for both Nietzsche and Epicurus, "the world can show itself as it is only when one steps out of the subjective, servile will and into the state of cessation of all need" (Vincenzo, 394). To feel oneself to be in the world and to embody its vital forces, is to "*realize in oneself* the eternal joy of becoming" (TI, "Ancients", 5).

> For Epicurus, *ataraxia* is an experience of the maximum pleasure of the aesthetic world and of oneself. It is a direct experience of the intrinsic pleasure of life itself, of the active forces of a life freed from the reactive force of desire. (Vincenzo 1994, 392)

The announcement of eternal return in section 341 of *The Gay Science* it is prefaced by "The Dying Socrates" (GS 340), a section in which Nietzsche presents his ultimate indictment of Platonism. Facing death, Socrates asks to make an offering to the god of medicine. The words, "O Crito, I owe Asclepius a rooster" betray his secret suffering of the "disease" of life (GS 340), his craven desire to live "beyond". In the wake of Platonism it may be necessary to "overcome even the Greeks" (GS 340) but an exception must be made for Epicurus, a fellow traveller of the earth. It is reputed that on the last day of his life Epicurus wrote to Hermarchus of his suffering and imminent death:

> I am suffering from diseases of the intestines and bladder which could not be more severe … However, all these sufferings are compensated by the joy of remembering our principles and our discoveries. […] My joy compensates the totality of pain. (Gaskin 1995, 66)

"The thought is clearly connected with the attitude expressed in Nietzsche's contemplation of the eternal recurrence; but this is not especially relevant to Nietzsche's view of Epicurus" (Bett 2005, 70).

Whatever torments they may each have known, there is no hint in the writings of Epicurus or of Nietzsche of ill will towards fate. Nietzsche to Peter Gast, 22nd January 1897:

> My health is abominable – rich in pain, like before; my life much more severe and lonely; I myself live on the whole almost like a complete saint, but almost with the disposition [Gesinnung] of the complete, genuine [ächt] Epicurus – very calm in soul and patient and yet watching life with joy (KSB, 5, 383).

When Nietzsche claims to experience the character of Epicurus differently to perhaps anyone else he feels a resurgence of the extraordinary affects of Epicurus, a stirring of the "past within". It seems likely that when he extolls the pleasures of the afternoon of antiquity he is recounting his rapturous experiences in the thought paths of St Moritz. This delight resurfaces on many an afternoon when on the rocky Genovese coast he lies like a lizard in the sun. The most serene possibility would be to live quietly and unknown, yet watching life with joy.

> To "want" something, to "strive" after something, to have a "goal", a "wish" in view – I do not know this from experience. Even at this moment I look out upon my future – a *vast* future! – as upon a smooth sea: it is ruffled by no desire. I do not want in the slightest that anything should become other than it is; I do not want myself to become other than I am. But that is how I have always lived. (EH, "Clever", 9)

Works Cited

Ansell Pearson, Keith. "True to the Earth: Nietzsche's Epicurean Care of Self and World" in *Nietzsche's Therapeutic Teaching: For Individuals and Culture*. Edited by Horst Hutter and Eli Friedland, London: Bloomsbury 2013, pp. 97-116. Print.

---."Heroic-idyllic philosophizing: Nietzsche and the Epicurean tradition". *Royal Institute of Philosophy Supplement*, 74, 2014, pp. 237-263. Available online at http://wrap.warwick.ac.uk/73448

Bett, Richard. "Nietzsche, the Greeks, and Happiness (with Special Reference to Aristotle and Epicurus)." *Philosophical Topics*. Vol. 33, No. 2, Fall 2005, pp. 45-70. Print.

Gaskin, John (ed.). *The Epicurean Philosophers*. London: Everyman, 1995. Print.

Hadot, Pierre. *Philosophy as a Way of Life: Spiritual Exercises from Socrates to Foucault*. Tr. By Michael Chase. Oxford: Blackwell, 1995. Print.

Krell, David Farrell and Bates, Donald L. *The Good European: Nietzsche's Work Sites in Word and Image*. Chicago: The University of Chicago Press, 1997. Print.

Nietzsche, F. *Nietzsche: Kritische Studienausgabe* in 15 volumes, edited by Giorgio Colli and Mazzino Montinari, Berlin : DTV/de Gruyter, 1967-77 and 1988. Print.

---.*Nietzsche: Sämtliche Briefe: Kritische Studienausgabe* in 8 volumes, edited by Giorgio Colli and Mazzino Montinari, Berlin : DTV/de Gruyter, 1975-1984 and 1986. Print.

Shearin, Wilson H., "Misunderstanding Epicurus: A Nietzschean Identification." *Journal of Nietzsche Studies*, Vol. 45, Issue 1, Spring 2014, pp. 68-83. Print.

Vincenzo, Joseph P. "Nietzsche and Epicurus" *Man and World*, Vol.27, No.4 (1994), pp. 383-397. Print.

Nietzsche's Joyful Friendship:
Epicurean Elements in the Middle Works

Willow Verkerk

In *The Gay Science* Nietzsche writes about the temperaments of Stoics and Epicureans stating that those whose "work is of the spirit" make "Epicurean arrangements." He writes:

> The Epicurean selects the situation, the persons, and even the events that suit his extremely irritable (*reizbaren*), intellectual constitution; he gives up all others, which means almost everything, because they would be too strong and heavy for him to digest. The Stoic, on the other hand, trains himself to swallow stones and worms, slivers of glass and scorpions without nausea; he wants his stomach to become ultimately indifferent to whatever the accidents of existence might pour into it […] For those with whom fate attempts improvisations—those who live in violent ages and depend on sudden and mercurial people—Stoicism may indeed be advisable. But anyone who foresees more or less that fate permits him to spin *a long thread* does well to make Epicurean arrangements. That is what all those have always done whose work is of the spirit (*alle Menschen der geistigen Arbeit*). For this type it would be the loss of losses to be deprived of their subtle irritability and be awarded in its place a hard Stoic hedgehog skin (GS §306).[1]

In Nietzsche's middle works one finds a definitely Epicurean mood in which Nietzsche seeks out, as specified in the above quote, the persons, situations, and events that will suit his contemplative irritability. Nietzsche's life during the free spirits trilogy of *Human all Too Human*, *Daybreak*, and *The Gay Science* was

---

[1] When quoting from Nietzsche's works, I use the following translations: Carol Diethe for "On the Genealogy of Morality," in *On the Genealogy of Morality and Other Writings*, (ed.) K. Ansell-Pearson, Cambridge, Cambridge University Press, 2008; Walter Kaufman for *The Gay Science*. New York, Vintage, 1974 and *Beyond Good and Evil*. New York, Vintage, 1966; R.J. Hollingdale for Volume 1 of *Human All Too Human*, "Assorted Opinions and Maxims" and "The Wanderer and His Shadow," in Volume 2, Cambridge: Cambridge University Press, 1986, and *Daybreak*. Cambridge: Cambridge University Press, 1997; Graham Parkes for *Thus Spoke Zarathustra*, Oxford, Oxford University Press, 2005; Judith Norman for "Ecce Homo," in *The Antichrist, Ecce Homo, Twilight of the Idols*. Cambridge, Cambridge University Press, 2005.

punctuated by illness and the need for convalescence which was then followed by periods of recovery in which Nietzsche wrote his texts. Although Nietzsche's struggles with sickness never left him, these experiences were relatively new to him during the free spirit writings of the middle period and allowed for a sensitivity to emerge in his work in which his writings become a search for moderation and companionship. One reason why the Nietzsche of the middle works has been too often neglected is that this Nietzsche is one who does not fit with the provocateur of the late period who performs cold rationality and active nihilism. In his own words, the late Nietzsche may be considered to have grown, through prolonged suffering, "a hard Stoic hedgehog skin."

The Nietzsche of the middle period is one who remains hopeful, one who wants to renew the Epicurean garden. In the free spirit writings Nietzsche can be recognized as sharing with Epicurus an emphasis on health, community, and freedom from the fear of death. Nietzsche's renewal or reinvention of the Epicurean garden is exemplified through his attempts to bring free spirits into being so that they can create a community that joins in friendship to share reflection and affirmation.

This essay elucidates how Nietzsche's middle period reflects a number of Epicurean elements specifically in regards to community and health through focusing on Nietzsche's free spirits as well as his praise of joyful friendship and its therapeutic role. I will argue that the joyful friendship is most celebrated by Nietzsche for its capacity to become a healing balm for the wounds of pity (*Mitleid*), which represent our more fundamental feeling of the fear of death. In Nietzsche's joyful friendship, the friends turn away from the burden of mortality and, in an Epicurean fashion, turn to the *lived* activities of the everyday to heal the self.

Nietzsche's Middle Works

Lou Salomé introduced the method of reading Nietzsche in periods as a practical way in which to connect his personal development with his writings and explain the diversity of his reflections;[2] it has since become a popular method in Nietzsche research. In general the periods are understood in the following way: the early period consists of Nietzsche's works from 1872-1876, the middle period is from 1878-1882, and the later works are those from 1883-1888. In addition to looking at the middle period, this essay turns to what may be considered

---

[2] Salomé, Lou. *Nietzsche*. Trans. Siegfried Mandel, Urbana and Chicago, University of Illinois Press, 2001. It was first published in German in 1894 as *Friedrich Nietzsche in Seinen Werke*.

Nietzsche's autobiographical works (which are part of his late period) in order to receive insight into the conceptual intentions of these books: this includes all of his prefaces and *Ecce Homo: How One Becomes What One Is*.[3]

Nietzsche's writings have a "living entelechy, in which later stages recuperate earlier ones and earlier ones hold in themselves all grounds of future unfolding."[4] For this reason, reading Nietzsche strictly in periods rather than approaching his texts as an oeuvre can be problematic. There are numerous examples in Nietzsche's text that support this supposition, one such example can be found in the preface to *On the Genealogy of Morality*:

> My thoughts on the descent of our moral prejudices - for that is what this polemic is about - were first set out in a sketchy and provisional way in the collection of aphorisms entitled *Human, All Too Human. A Book for Free Spirits*, which I began to write in Sorrento during a winter that enabled me to pause, like a wanderer pauses, to take in the vast and dangerous land through which my mind had hitherto travelled. This was in the winter of 1876-7; the thoughts themselves go back further. They were mainly the same thoughts which I shall be taking up again in the present essays - let us hope that the long interval has done them good, that they have become riper, brighter, stronger and more perfect! (GM P§2)

What is also important to note is that in the same preface, Nietzsche states that in order to understand his *Genealogy*, one must have read his earlier texts (GM P§8). These proclamations of Nietzsche's demonstrate that he considers his works to have an overarching project that is developed over time. From the above quotation one might argue that there is a refinement of ideas that occurs in Nietzsche's later works; however this should not discount his earlier writings from being taken on their own terms. Nietzsche considers his yes-saying work, characteristic of the middle period, to be just as important as his later no-saying work for achieving a transformation of culture. It is in the free spirits texts along with *Thus Spoke Zarathustra* that Nietzsche reveals how vital one's life praxis and social relationship are to one's philosophical work for achieving a re-evaluation of values.

In the middle works, Nietzsche is bringing a probity to his philosophy that is motivated by what he considers to be the "profits" (*Gewinn*) given to him by his

---

[3] Translation modified. The German is, *Wie man wird, was man ist*

[4] Hutter, Horst. *Shaping The Future: Nietzsche's New Regime of the Soul and Its Ascetic Practices*. Oxford, Lexington Books, 2006, p. 4.

experience of prolonged illness (GS P§3). These profits include new philosophical ideas such as the free spirit, which he states that he conceives to act as his imaginative companions during difficult times (HH I P§2). Nietzsche links his generative notion of suffering to Epicurus when he states that he experiences Epicurus differently from other people. Of Epicurus Nietzsche writes,

> Such happiness could be invented only by a man who was suffering continually. It is the happiness of eyes that have seen the sea of existence become calm, and now they can never weary of the surface and of the many hues of this tender, shuddering skin of the sea. Never before has voluptuousness been so modest (GS §45).

In an Epicurean sense, Nietzsche is stating that human frailty and mortality should not deter us from enjoyment; instead, knowledge of our human limits should reinvigorate us to pursue the pleasures of life with intelligence and modesty. Epicurus writes in his letter to Menoeceus, "a correct understanding that death is nothing to us makes the mortality of life enjoyable, not by adding infinite time, but by ridding us of the desire for immortality." [5] As one commentator points out, the Greeks of antiquity took the precariousness of life as a given; what Epicurus brought to this familiarity was its ability to inspire action.[6]

The capacity to come to terms with one's mortality allows for life to be infused with an enthusiasm in which one recognizes following Epicurus that "to practice living well and to practice dying well are one and the same."[7] According to Keith Ansell-Pearson, Nietzsche is able to evoke an important aspect of Epicurus's thinking, namely that even though we suffer, this life is the only life for us and it is "worthy of our attachment and affirmation": this in turn helps us to accept the inevitability of our place within the world so that we can find meaning here within the pleasures and delights that it offers.[8]

The reminder of one's mortality through suffering is generative not only because, as Nietzsche writes, "we have to give birth to our thoughts out of our pain" (GS P§3), but also because it allows for us to focus our attention to the

---

[5] Long, A.A & D.N. Sedley. *The Hellenistic philosophers vol. 1 Translations of the Principal Sources with Philosophical Commentary*. Cambridge, Cambridge University Press, 1987, p.149.
[6] DeWitt, Norman Wentworth. *Epicurus and his Philosophy*. Minneapolis: University of Minnesota Press, 1954, p.183.
[7] Ibid., p.150.
[8] Ansell-Pearson, Keith. "Heroic-idyllic philosophizing : Nietzsche and the Epicurean tradition." *Royal Institute of Philosophy Supplement* 74, 2014, pp.237-263, 263.

lived experience of the everyday. Through the middle works we can see that Nietzsche develops and introduces core aspects of his substantive philosophical thinking as life philosophy with a therapeutic Epicurean aim.

Human All Too Human is considered the start of Nietzsche's middle period because it indicates his initiation into aphoristic writing and his own declaration that with this text, he freed himself from ideals that were no longer meaningful to him. He writes:

> *Human, All Too Human* is the monument to a crisis. It calls itself a book for *free* spirits: almost every sentence is the manifestation of a victory – I used it to liberate myself from things that *did not belong* to my nature. Idealism is one of them: the title says 'where *you* see ideal things, I see - human, oh, only all too human!' (EH "Human All Too Human" §1).

Nietzsche is referring to his disenchantment with and disconnection from Schopenhauer and Wagner, as well as his move away from Romanticism toward a more scientific approach to knowledge-seeking inspired by Paul Rée. In *Human* Nietzsche problematizes morality for being unegoisitc and, in doing so, writes to demonstrate the impossibility of this kind of morality. He invents the notion of the free spirit as a therapeutic model as well as a replacement for those persons and ideals he has abandoned. He views free spirits as his future friends and writes about them with the intention of bringing them into existence (HH I P§2).

The two spiritual objectives of *Human* are made explicit by Nietzsche during his later reflections on the book when he states that *Assorted Opinions and Maxims* and *The Wanderer and his Shadow* are "a continuation and redoubling of a spiritual cure, namely of the anti-romantic self-treatment that my still healthy instinct had itself discovered and prescribed for me against a temporary attack of the most dangerous form of romanticism" (HH II P§2). He states that these texts contain principles for those inclined toward self-discipline and spiritual health (HH II P§2). In addition to being an early analysis of our collective moral prejudices that is developed in *Daybreak* and *Genealogy*, *Human* is a text that is profoundly therapeutic with the aim of transforming both the author and its readers through its constructive, yes-saying ethics of the free spirit.

To become free Nietzsche writes that one must experiment with conflicting beliefs (HH I P§4), employ the "almost cheerful and inquisitive coldness of the psychologist" (HH II P§1), and be prepared to suffer and renounce former things that were once highly valued (HH I P§4; HH I P§6). Nietzsche states that this process includes periods of convalescence and it is very painful, but one is propelled onward by "a *tenacious* will to health" (HH I P§4). Although *Human* is a yes-saying book, Nietzsche enacts the no-saying voice when he undermines the values associated with the Christian-Platonic moral heritage and its desire for an afterlife. For Nietzsche, no-saying is an implicit part of yes-saying required for re-evaluation. In *Human*, Nietzsche avoids a destructive atmosphere, more characteristic of his later no-saying texts like *Beyond Good and Evil*, by his notion of the free spirit who becomes the figure of possibility for a more individuated ethical approach to life.

Daybreak: Thoughts on the Prejudices of Morality is a more enthusiastic yes-saying text than *Human*. Nietzsche writes that *Daybreak* supports a contradiction that he is unafraid of: "faith in morality is withdrawn" but this very withdrawal is motivated by a moral perspective. What is occurring, is "the self-sublimation of morality" (D P§4). In *Daybreak*, as well as the other middle period texts, Nietzsche is attempting to make the ethical life more joyful. Although self-becoming involves much discipline and habituation, Nietzsche aims to transform morality into an Epicurean ethics of self-cultivation in which the individual enjoys the process of becoming what one is.[9]

Nietzsche is a "subterranean man" (D P§1) in this text who destabilizes moral precepts, but he does so with an affirmative style that celebrates a future in which values will be re-written (EH "Daybreak" §1). In fact, with this text he is already introducing the notion that there are many moralities, that there need not be one overarching unegoistic morality.[10] Nietzsche encourages his readers to experiment with different kinds of life practices, practices which are self-affirmative (D §453), to test out new variations of moralities (D §164), and to focus on self-concern in the construction of one's own ethics.

One of the central goals of *Daybreak* is to help individuals recognize the "morality of custom" that indoctrinates them into collective systems of values in which their individual needs are subjected to the interests of society. This is certainly a continuation of the earlier project initiated in *Human* to help "fettered spirits" become free. Regarding the project of *Daybreak* Nietzsche writes, "The loss of a center of gravity, resistance to natural instincts, in a word 'selflessness'—this is what has been called 'morality' so far . . . In *Daybreak* I first took up the fight against the morality of 'unselfing.'" (EH "Daybreak" §2).

Nietzsche states that just as *Daybreak* is a yes-saying book, so is *The Gay Science*, but to the "highest degree" (EH "The Gay Science"). He uses the words "triumph," "gratitude," "hope," and "intoxication" to describe the "rejoicing of

---

[9] Ansell-Pearson, Keith. "Beyond compassion: on Nietzsche's moral therapy in *Dawn*." *Continental Philosophy Review* 44, 2011, pp.179-204, 180.

[10] Ansell-Pearson, "Beyond compassion: on Nietzsche's moral therapy in *Dawn*," p. 182.

strength" of this book (GS P§1). In this text, Nietzsche's voice as a passionate and affirmative knowledge-seeker is most vibrant. He approaches philosophical problems from the perspective of a physician of culture[11] who wants to help both individual and cultural development. In the preface he states that he is "waiting for a philosophical physician in the exceptional sense of the word—one who has to pursue the problem of the total health of a people, time, race, or of humanity" (GS P§2).

Nietzsche situates himself as a psychologist in the preface of *Gay Science* when he states that a psychologist is fascinated by the relationship between health and philosophy. He writes that when a psychologist becomes ill he will adopt a scientific curiosity toward that illness from which he suffers (GS P§2). Nietzsche places a value on the learning potential that comes out of suffering and illness and even claims that one who has suffered will pursue knowledge with less reservation. Out of suffering arises a person with more questions and a will to question more severely: "The trust in life is gone: life itself has become a *problem*. Yet one should not jump to the conclusion that this necessarily makes one gloomy." In fact, Nietzsche thinks that a philosopher who has suffered much and practiced self-mastery to endure is likely to become more attracted to that which is most problematic and unknown, to become open to trying out and even enjoying multiple perspectives (GS P§3).

Having recently come out of an illness prior to the writing of this book, in *The Gay Science* Nietzsche is attempting to think about how truth is shaped, not only by health/illness, but also by what is 'useful' (GS §110). Nietzsche claims that what is needed for the pursuit of knowledge is a "philosophical *physician*" that will inquire as to what is "at stake" in the philosophy in question, not the naïve objectivity of 'truth,' but instead an awareness of how "health, future, growth, power, life" (GS P§2) shape our belief systems. The very title of this book points to the connection between truth and artistry. Nietzsche's goal is to make the pursuit of knowledge or science as a life practice more joyful and to teach his free spirits about the construction of truth so that they can understand it and learn to employ these practices for the creation of their own values and truths.

---

[11] Citing *The Gay Science* (P§2), Van Tongeren claims that Nietzsche approaches philosophy as "a physician of culture," both as a psychologist and a physiologist. Nietzsche did so because he was influenced by the medical Greek approach to doing philosophy and also because he endured much suffering through illness in his life and his philosophical approach was admittedly affected by this. Van Tongeren, Paul. *Reinterpreting Modern Culture*. West Lafayette, Indiana, Purdue University Press, 2000, pp. 2-3.

A Community of Free Spirits

In 1879 Nietzsche wrote letters to his friends Peter Gast and Paul Rée in which he expressed interest in starting his own Epicurean garden (KSB 5 399, 460). In his reflections on the middle period, Nietzsche suggests that the free spirit describes those friends that he would like himself to have, people who have or who are attempting to disconnect with the conventions that are most familiar to them. These people will need new friends who can understand what is at stake and provide each other space for repose. In reflecting on his mood while writing *Human*, Nietzsche points to his desire to find friends with whom to share the simple pleasures removed from the noise of society.

> What I again and again needed most for my cure and self-restoration, however, was the belief that I was not thus isolated, not alone in seeing as I did—an enchanted surmising of relatedness and identity in eye and desires, a reposing in a trust of friendship, a blindness in concert with another without suspicion or question-marks, a pleasure in foregrounds, surfaces, things close and closest, in everything possessing color, skin and apparitionality (HH I §P1).

One cannot help but think of Epicurus's sentiment: "The purest security is that which comes from a quiet life and withdrawal from the many."[12] In *The Gay Science* Nietzsche expresses his frustration with how leisure has come to be perceived of as idleness, stating that we are approaching a time in which people will not be able to enjoy contemplative moments with one's ideas or one's friends without succumbing to a feeling a "bad conscience" (GS §329). For Nietzsche, if one wants to enjoy a contemplative life one must find ways to remove oneself from the world and join together with other like-minded people who are not fettered but free.

Nietzsche distinguishes the free spirit from the fettered spirit by placing them into opposition to one another, stating that the fettered sprit follows habit and seeks out experiences that re-assert their habituated beliefs (HH §225). On the other hand, the free spirit pursues the exception to the rule and is themselves an exception to the rule which is obtained through inquiry, reason, and liberation away from tradition (HH §225). Nietzsche emphasizes that the free spirit is someone whose beliefs and way of life differ from the majority and more specifically from their class, profession, origins, and environment (HH §225).

---

[12] Inwood, Brad and L.P. Gerson. *The Epicurus Reader*. Indiannapolis/Cambridge, Hackett Publishing, 1994, p.33.

Does Nietzsche mean to open up his hope for a shared community of free spirits to women and people from various kinds of backgrounds?

Epicurus did not restrict his teachings to men or the youth, his teachings were for people, both men and women of all ages, "whether slave or free."[13] For this reason, one would be inclined to suppose that Nietzsche's reinvention of the Epicurean garden would embrace all people, in his own words, "who think differently from[…]the dominant views of the age" (HH §225). However, this is not exactly the case for Nietzsche because, according to him, the free spirit cannot be ideologically enslaved and he believes that this is the general predicament of women.

Nietzsche writes that although women are attracted to free spirited endeavors, they have been socialized "for millennia" to be subservient to societal authorities more than men (HH §435). The feminine inclination to service (HH §432) in conjunction with the social position of women that Nietzsche writes is one of slavery (GM III§18 and Z I "On the Friend") makes it extremely difficult for women to become free spirits. Nevertheless, if we approach Nietzsche's notion of the free spirit specifically in terms of how he describes it in *Human* (§225), exceptional women should be able to become free spirits through the progressive emancipation from those traditional roles to which they are subjected (HH §225).

Nietzsche characterizes free spirits as those who pursue probity through demanding reasons for their beliefs (HH §225). In doing so, they question their attachments to their convictions and habits and relinquish the certitudes of faith (HH §226; GS §347). I have argued elsewhere that agonistic friendship is central to the process of overcoming required to become a free spirit.[14] However, in the middle texts the kind of friendship most emphasized by Nietzsche, and connecting to the building of a Epicurean inspired community, is one of joy in which free spirits come together to experience pleasure through shared reflection and self-affirmation.

The Joyful Friendship as a Healing Balm

In *The Vatican Collection of Epicurean Sayings* we can read the following: "Friendship dances around the world announcing to all of us that we must wake up to blessedness."[15] The joyful aspect of friendship that is accentuated by Epicurus is taken up by Nietzsche in the free spirits texts when he writes that

---

[13] DeWitt, *Epicurus and his Philosophy*, Minneapolis, University of Minnesota Press, 1954, p.29.

[14] Verkerk, Willow. "Nietzsche's Agonistic Ethics of Friendship." *Symposium: Canadian Journal for Continental Philosophy* 20.2, Fall 2016, pp.22-41.

[15] Inwood, *The Epicurus Reader*, 1994, p.38.

friends should share joy not suffering (GS §338) and states: "Fellow rejoicing (*Mitfreude*), not fellow suffering (*Mitleiden*) makes the friend" (HH §499). The importance of sharing joy is further emphasized by Nietzsche in *Daybreak* (§422) as a life activating principle that creates a feeling of fullness in the individual. This shared feeling of fullness is a remedy for the sicknesses of the modern human soul such as pity, guilt, and consumerism.

In *The Gay Science* (§338) Nietzsche encourages those who seek "one's own way" (free spirits) to separate themselves from society and even to "live in seclusion." He qualifies this by stating that it is sure that one will want to share community and help others, but one should help only one's friends who "share with you one suffering and one hope" and in doing so help oneself. Nietzsche ends this section by proclaiming in response to the "preachers of pity: *to share not suffering but joy*" (GS §338). Nietzsche is outlining the significance of the joyful friendship in terms of its ability to act as a healing balm for the experiences of pity.

Nietzsche thinks that the expression of pity hides more self-serving motivations that seek to overpower the other or to turn away from one's own fear of suffering (D §133; HH §103) and with this the fear of death. He also thinks that one who demands pity may in fact be motivated not by the desire to be cared for but instead by the desire to hurt someone else (HH §50). Pity, associated with care and kindness, is often a cloaked expression of egoism according to Nietzsche. The burden of pity is one which is self-destructive.

> *Why double your 'ego'!*—To view our own experiences with the eyes with which we are accustomed to view them when they are the experiences of others—this is very comforting and a medicine to be recommended. On the other hand, to view and imbibe the experience of others *as if they were ours*—as is the demand of a philosophy of pity (*Philosophie des Mitleidens*) —this would destroy us, and in a very short time (D §137).

Pity (*Mitleid*) or suffering-with, is a likely reaction to the suffering of another person, but Nietzsche considers it to be an inevitable strain by frustrating the one who is being pitied. Nietzsche views pity to be a largely disabling and reductive perspective that fails to adequately acknowledge the situation and feelings of the suffering friend. On the most shallow level, there is a condescension involved in the expression of pity ('poor you') that disempowers the friend, promotes an atmosphere of hopelessness, and a nihilistic attitude toward life. The individual experience of suffering cannot be grasped by another person, yet sometimes the one who pities presumes that they can and thus does so superficially. When they make the move to 'help' the friend, they do so with an idea in mind that is so results-driven in its impatience that it overlooks the friend's actual struggle. Rather than being motivated by care for the friend, Nietzsche states that pity is moved by a fear that wants to abolish suffering (BGE §225). At the core of pity is a perspective on life that is dominated by the need to avoid all pain and discomfort, which are inevitably reminders of one's mortality. Generally speaking, Nietzsche thinks that people are too anxious about their mortality (D §174). Behind the pity that one experiences for the friend is an anxiety about death. One wants the friend to feel better, but they want the friend to feel better because the friend's suffering is disturbing. This dismissive gesture lacks sympathy, or a genuine attempt to feel-with (*Mitgefühl*) the friend and respect their struggle.

What one requires is the development of an Epicurean attitude that will counteract the tendency toward pity that Nietzsche thinks people of modernity share. In *The Wanderer and his Shadow*, Nietzsche refers to two kinds of Epicurean "consolation" to help one accept the ways things are (WS §7) and in *Daybreak* he recommends an alternative to approaching the friend with pity. Nietzsche asks whether it is more useful to help another person by "immediately leaping to his side" which can itself become an overpowering act in which one attempts to exert their own will upon the other. Perhaps it might be more helpful to create "something out of oneself that the other can behold with pleasure: a beautiful, restful, self-enclosed garden perhaps, with high walls against storms and the dust of the roadway but also a hospital gate" (D §174). Following Epicurus, we should "share our friends' suffering not with laments but with thoughtful concern."[16]

This essay has attempted to illuminate Epicurean elements in Nietzsche's middle works through a study of the free spirit and the therapeutic aspects of Nietzsche's joyful friendship. For Epicurus, friendship takes one away from the pain of human mortality and toward tranquility through the community and security it provides.[17] In Nietzsche's joyful friendship, free spirits become less anxious about their mortality through enabling each other to express and share joy. The community that they hold together provides a healing balm for the realities of human life, one which allows for the activation of an affirmative energy. "Why is making joyful the greatest of all joys?—Because we thereby give joy to our fifty separate drives all at once. Individually they may be very little joys:

---

[16] *The Epicurus Reader*, p.39.

[17] In *The Principal Doctrines* of Diogenes Laertius, one can find the following: "The same understanding produces confidence about there being nothing terrible which is eternal of [even] long-lasting and has also realized that security amid even these limited [bad things] is most easily achieved through friendship." *The Epicurus Reader*, p.34.

but if we take them all into one hand, our hand is fuller than at any other time—
and our heart too!" (D §422)

Works Cited

Ansell-Pearson, Keith. "Beyond compassion: on Nietzsche's moral therapy in Dawn." *Continental Philosophy Review* 44, 2011, pp.179-204

— "Heroic-idyllic philosophizing : Nietzsche and the Epicurean tradition." *Royal Institute of Philosophy Supplement* 74, 2014, pp.237-263.

DeWitt, Norman Wentworth. *Epicurus and his Philosophy*. Minneapolis: University of Minnesota Press, 1954.

Hutter, Horst. *Shaping The Future: Nietzsche's New Regime of the Soul and Its Ascetic Practices*. Oxford, Lexington Books, 2006.

Inwood, Brad and L.P. Gerson. *The Epicurus Reader*. Indiannapolis/Cambridge, Hackett Publishing, 1994.

Nietzsche, Friedrich. *The Antichrist, Ecce Homo, Twilight of the Idols*. Translated by Judith Norman. Cambridge, Cambridge University Press, 2005.

— *Beyond Good and Evil*. Translated by Walter Kaufmann. New York, Vintage 1966.

—*Daybreak*. Translated by R.J. Hollingdale. Cambridge, Cambridge University Press, 1997.

—*The Gay Science*. Translated by Walter Kaufmann. New York, Vintage, 1974.

—*Human All Too Human*. Translated by R.J. Hollingdale. Cambridge, Cambridge University Press, 1986.

—*On the Genealogy of Morality*. Translated by Carol Diethe, Edited by Keith Ansell-Pearson. Cambridge, Cambridge University Press, 1994.

—*Thus Spoke Zarathustra*. Translated by Graham Parkes. Oxford, Oxford University Press, 2005.

Salomé, Lou. *Nietzsche*. Translated by Siegfried Mandel, Urbana and Chicago, University of Illinois Press, 2001.

Long, A.A & D.N. Sedley. *The Hellenistic philosophers vol. 1 Translations of the Principal Sources with Philosophical Commentary*. Cambridge, Cambridge University Press, 1987.

Van Tongeren, Paul. *Reinterpreting Modern Culture*. West Lafayette, Indiana, Purdue University Press, 2000.

Verkerk, Willow. "Nietzsche's Agonistic Ethics of Friendship." *Symposium: Canadian Journal for Continental Philosophy* 20.2, Fall 2016, pp.22-41.

On Nietzsche's Search for Happiness and Joy:
Thinking with Epicurus

Keith Ansell-Pearson

Believe me, real joy is a serious matter (Seneca, 23rd Letter to Lucilius).

As Richard Bett has noted, Nietzsche likes to give the impression that he is against happiness altogether.[1] A well-known aphorism in a late text, *Twilight of the Idols*, is typical in this regard: "Humanity does not strive for happiness; only the English do that" (TI "Maxims and Arrows", 12).[2] However, an examination of Nietzsche, especially of the neglected middle period texts, can show that he is deeply concerned with the fate of happiness and also that he develops rich conceptions of pleasure and joy. In the following I explore various renditions of happiness and joy in Nietzsche's writings, offering a series of perspectives on the topic. I want to begin with an aphorism from *The Gay Science*, number, 45, and simply entitled "Epicurus." It is a reflection on the happiness of the afternoon of antiquity; so let me begin there.

The Happiness of the Afternoon of Antiquity[3]
Nietzsche writes that he is proud of the fact that he experiences the character of Epicurus differently from perhaps everybody else: "Whatever I hear or read of him, I enjoy the happiness of the afternoon of antiquity." In this aphorism, simply entitled "Epicurus," Nietzsche writes:

---

[1] Richard Bett, "Nietzsche, the Greeks, and Happiness' 45—70, 45.

[2] Nietzsche, *Twilight of the Idols*, trans. Duncan Large.

[3] My appreciation of this aphorism from *The Gay Science* was greatly enriched by the graduate seminar I taught on Nietzsche at Warwick University in the spring term of 2013, and especially the contributions of Robert Kron and Jeffrey Pickernell. Thanks also for inspiration to Beatrice Han-Pile and Rainer Hanshe; for assistance with the translation of the essay by Richard Roose I extend my thanks to Frank Chouraqui.

I see his eyes gaze upon a wide, white sea, across rocks at the shore that are bathed in sunlight, while large and small animals are playing in this light, as secure and calm as the light and his eyes. Such happiness could be invented only by a man who was suffering continually. It is the happiness of eyes that have seen the sea of existence become calm, and now they can never weary of the surface and of the many hues of this tender, shuddering skin of the sea. Never before has voluptuousness (*Wollust*) been so modest.[4]

As Monika Langer has noted in her interpretation of this aphorism, although clearly a paean of sorts to Epicurus, Nietzsche does not elaborate on the origin or nature of his happiness and suffering, but rather tacitly encourages the reader to consider various possibilities. In the end she argues that Nietzsche is reading Epicurus as a figure who whilst standing securely on firm ground, gazes at the sea and is able to enjoy the possibility of uncertainty it offers. She writes, "Literally and figuratively he can float on the sea."[5] Epicurus is depicted as the antithesis of modernity's shipwrecked man since such is his liberation and serenity he can "chart his course or simply set sail and let the wind determine his way."[6] Although he might suffer shipwreck and drown or survive he does not live in fear of dangers and hazards: "In taking to the sea he might lose his bearings and even his mind." In contrast to modern man who is keen to leave behind the insecurity of the sea for the safety of dry land, "Epicurus delights in the ever present possibility of leaving that secure land for the perils of the sea."[7]

This interpretation misses the essential insight Nietzsche is developing into Epicurus in the aphorism. Rather than suggesting that the sea calls for further and continued exploration, hiding seductive dangers that Epicurus would not be afraid of, Nietzsche seems to hold to the view that Epicurus is the seasoned traveller of the soul who has no desire to travel anymore and for whom the meaning of the sea has changed. Rather than serving as a means of transportation or something that beckons us towards other shores, the sea has become an object

---

[4] *The Gay Science*, translated Walter Kaufmann (new York: Random House, 1974), section 45. For insight into the "distinctly Genoese" character of the Epicuruean bliss Nietzsche is writing about in this aphorism see Martina Kolb, Martina Kolb's study, *Nietzsche, Freud, Benn, and the Azure Spell of Liguria* (Toronto: University of Toronto Press, 2013), 113. She sees Nietzsche's gay science as "an admixture of Greek serenity combined with various psycho-poetic Provençalisms" (ibid.). She further writes that it is in Genoa, Liguria, "that Nietzsche finds self-sufficiency, self-liberation, self-love..." (114).
[5] Monika M. Langer, *Nietzsche's Gay Science: Dancing Coherence*, 67.
[6] Ibid.
[7] Ibid.

of contemplation in the here and now. It is something to be looked at for its own sake and in a way that discloses its infinite nuances and colours. The scene Nietzsche depicts is one of Epicurean illumination or enlightenment: Epicurus is not estranged from nature and recognizes his kinship with animals and the elements of nature. Rather than deploying his contemplation of the sea to bolster his own ego (thinking of his own safety or taking pride in fearlessness), Epicurus abandons his sense of self altogether so that he can open himself up to the sea of existence. Unlike Christ, Epicurus does not walk on the water but floats serenely on the sea, buoyed up by it and even cradled by it, happy with the gifts life has to offer, and existing beyond fear and anxiety even though he is opening himself up to troubling realities, such as the approach of death and his personal extinction: "We are born once and cannot be born twice, but we must be no more for all time."[8] As Langer rightly notes, the imagery deployed in the aphorism is striking: far from evoking boredom the serenity of Epicurus signals a kind of ecstatic bliss.[9]

In *The Gay Science* 45 Nietzsche makes a specific contribution to our understanding of Epicurean happiness or ataraxia. According to the portrait of Epicurus he provides this happiness is hard-won and has a precarious character, being inseparable from suffering: the sea of existence has become calm but, as Bett puts it, "its continued calmness cannot be guaranteed, and the "shuddering skin of the sea" is a constant reminder of the turmoil that may return."[10]

Heroic-Idyllic

Another paean to Epicurus from the middle period can be found in the earlier text, *The Wanderer and his Shadow*. In aphorism 295 Nietzsche depicts an idyllic scene entitled "*Et in Arcadia ego*," involving looking down "over waves of hills, through fir-trees and spruce trees grave with age, towards a milky green lake."[11] Whilst cattle graze on their own, and gather in groups, the narrator of the aphorism experiences, "everything at peace in the contentment of evening." Whilst looking upon the herders in the field, he witnesses mountain slopes and snowfields to the left and, high above him, to the right two gigantic ice-covered peaks that seem to float in a veil of sunlit vapour: "everything big, still and bright" (ibid.). The beauty of the whole scene induces in him an experience of the sublime, "a sense of awe and of adoration of the moment of its revelation"; involuntarily, as if completely natural, he inserts "into this pure, clear world of

---

[8] Epicurus, "Vatican Sayings," number 14.
[9] Langer, *Nietzsche's Gay Science*, 67.
[10] Richard Bett, "Nietzsche, the Greeks, and Happiness", 63.
[11] Nietzsche, *The Wanderer and His Shadow* in *Human, all too Human*, volume two, trans. Gary Handwerk, 295.

light," free of desire and expectation, with no looking before or behind, Hellenic heroes, and he compares the feeling to that of Poussin and his pupil (probably Claude Lorrain), at one and the same time heroic and idyllic, noting to himself that some human beings have actually *lived* in accordance with this experience, having "enduringly *felt* they existed in the world and the world existed in them" (ibid.).[12] Epicurus is singled out for special mention.

The title of this aphorism is borrowed from two paintings of Poussin and was also adopted by Goethe as the motto of his Italian journey (1829). In fact, Poussin's paintings were inspired by Guercino (Giovanni Francesco Barbieri) and his painting of around 1618-22 entitled "Et in Arcadia ego." This painting depicts the discovery of death in Arcady, a region of Greece thought to be an earthly paradise: we see two shepherds gazing out of a wood at a skull that has been placed on a masonry plinth, and underneath the skull the inscription "Et in Arcadia ego" can be read. Such words seem to be intended as a message spoken by death itself, "I, Death, am also in Arcady."[13]

There are several striking things about Nietzsche's turn to, and portrait of, the idyllic. First, we can note the contrast with his earlier critique of the idyll in *The Birth of Tragedy* where it is equated with the superficial and the optimistic (BT 8, 19). Second, in his depiction of the heroic-idyllic scene the reality of death is completely absent from it. What might be informing Nietzsche's decision to leave death out of the picture is the Epicurean inspiration that the fear of death has been conquered and death is nothing to us.[14] Thus, Nietzsche does not wish the image of the tombstone to cast a shadow over the idyll he is focusing our attention on: for this reason it is both heroic and idyllic. And third, for Nietzsche the idyll is not in any inaccessible celestial heavens but belongs in this world and is within

---

[12] One might even see in this contemplation of nature, where all is peace and calm and where we have moved beyond "desire and expectation," something of Schopenhauer's ideas on art, including the release from the subjectivity of the will. Schopenhauer, in fact, depicted such a state in Epicurean terms: 'Then all at once the peace, always sought but always escaping us on that first path of willing, comes to us of its own accord, and all is well with us. It is the painless state, prized by Epicurus as the highest good and as the state of the gods; for that moment we are delivered from the miserable pressure of the will.' Schopenhauer, *The World as Will and Representation*, volume one, section 38,196. See also Schopenhauer on the "aesthetic delight" to be had from the experience of light: "Light is most pleasant and delightful; it has become the symbol of all that is good and salutary," 199.

[13] Henry Keazor, *Poussin*, p. 57. See also Erwin Panofsky, "*Et in Arcadia Ego*: Poussin and the Elegiac Tradition," *Meaning in the Visual Arts* (Middlesex: Penguin, 1987), 340-67.

[14] Richard Bett, "Nietzsche, the Greeks, and Happiness," 65.

our reach, and what takes place after death does not concern us anymore.[15] Nietzsche writes in *Dawn*: "…the after-death no longer concerns us! An unspeakable blessing…and once again, Epicurus triumphs!" (D 72)[16]

The heroic-idyllic is heroic, then, at least in part, because conquering the fear of death is involved and the human being has the potential to walk on the earth as a god, living a blessed life, and idyllic because Epicurus philosophised, calmly and serenely, and away from the crowd, in a garden. In *Human, all too Human* Nietzsche writes of a refined heroism, "which disdains to offer itself to the veneration of the great masses…and goes silently through the world and out of the world" (HH 291).[17] This is deeply Epicurean in inspiration: Epicurus taught that one should die as if one had never lived. There is a modesty of human existence in Epicurean teaching that greatly appeals to the middle period Nietzsche.

The garden appeals to Nietzsche in his middle writings as a place of contemplation and relaxation. He wants a new *vita contemplativa* to be cultivated in the midst of the speed and rapidity of modern life; we need to slow down, to go slowly, and to create the time needed to work through our experiences. Even we godless anti-metaphysicians need places for contemplation and in which we can reflect on ourselves and encounter ourselves. However, we are not to do this in the typical spiritual manner of transcendent loftiness, but rather take walks in botanical gardens, the gardens that will replace the churches of old, and look at ourselves translated, as Nietzsche memorably puts it, into stones and plants (GS 280). We free spirits have more in common with phenomena of the natural world than we do with the heavenly projections of a religious humanity: we can be blissfully silent like stones and we have specific conditions of growth like plants, being nourished by the elements of the earth and by the light and heat of the sun.

The Happiness of the Free Spirit

What kind of happiness does the free spirit seek? In *Human, all too Human* Nietzsche writes of "the desire for a blissful, serene mobility" as the philosopher's – and artist's - vision of happiness (HH 611). Indeed, a few aphorisms before this one he notes how human beings construct for themselves "gardens of happiness" in the midst of the sorrow of the world and upon its volcanic ground. They do

---

[15] Richard Roos, "Nietzsche et Épicure: l'idylle héroïque," 283-350, 322.

[16] Nietzsche, *Dawn: Thoughts on the Presumptions of Morality*, trans. Brittain Smith (Stanford: Stanford University Press, 2011).

[17] Nietzsche, *Human, all too Human*, trans. Gary Handwerk (Stanford: Stanford University Press, 1995).

this in multiple ways, be it in the manner of someone who observes life and has the eye for wanting knowledge from existence, or of someone who submits and resigns himself to life, or of a person who rejoices in their overcoming of the difficulties of life: in each case of happiness sprouts beside the misfortune (HH 591). The longing for "blissful" and "serene" mobility seems to provide the kind of happiness or joy sought by the wandering free spirit prized in the middle period texts, and anticipates something of the character of the joyful wisdom of the gay science. Of course, Nietzsche does not have a univocal conception of happiness and severely criticizes one form of happiness in particular, which he finds contemptible because it rests on a smug ease and amounts to a religion of comfortableness (see GS 318 & 338). It is against this kind of happiness that Nietzsche advises his readers to build their houses on the slopes of Mt Vesuvius and to live dangerously. In *The Gay Science*, and as we have seen, Nietzsche notes how the happiness of Epicurus is born out of suffering from existence, and yet it is this suffering that makes its precarious attainment something meaningful. Further in this text he notes how the happiness of Homer's soul is a "melancholy happiness"; it is one that makes you more liable to suffering, simply because there is the fact that one may lose it at any time and in which just a little displeasure and loathing will suffice in the end to make you disgusted with life (GS 302).[18] The idea of loss and mourning is continued in the next aphorism where Nietzsche perceptively writes of the worth and sum of life as meaning more for the person who knows more of life precisely because they have been so often on the verge of losing it, and so they have "*more* of life" than those who have never had this experience. This is a kind of joy and happiness in life that is, in fact, based on experience and as something actually lived. Perhaps the highest kind of personal happiness Nietzsche prizes is the one described in *The Gay Science* 326. Here Nietzsche attacks preachers of morality, as well as theologians, for painting a too dramatic portrait of the human condition in which the human animal is portrayed in fatally sick terms and the only cure for its malaise is a radical and final one: the pain and misfortune of existence are painted in a far too exaggerated manner. Instead, Nietzsche favours the capacities individuals have for overcoming and conquering their pains and misfortunes, pouring sweetness on their bitterness, and finding remedies in their bravery and sublimity: all of this can give rise to new forms of strength. The happiness of the free spirit appears to be one of an "eternal liveliness" (WS 350), in which one is open to new experiences and that allow for

---

[18] On melancholy see also GS 291 and 337.

the emergence of new sources of strength and maturation, and also make one attentive to the complex needs of our bodily and spiritual economy.

In aphorism 309 of *The Gay Science* entitled "From the Seventh Solitude," Nietzsche writes of the wanderer as being driven by a penchant and passion of for the true – for the real, the non-apparent, and the certain – and that allows no rest and that perpetually seduces him to tarry. Although the gardens of Armida beckon he must keep tearing his heart away so to experience *new* bitternesses, and so he goes on since he "must go on," even if it is with weary and wounded feet and looking back in wrath at the most beautiful things that could not detain him and because they could not detain him.

The deployment in the aphorism of wounded feet may be a reference to Sophocles' play *Philoctetes*. Philoctetes has been bequeathed a bow by Heracles and becomes a master of the weapon and sets forth against Troy with some companions, including Agamemnon. On the way to Troy, however, he and his companions make a stop at an island so as to make a sacrifice to the local deity. As he approaches the shrine Philoctetes is bitten in the foot by a snake, and as the infection becomes virulent his groans mean that it becomes impossible to make the sacrifice, as the act would be ruined by these ill-omened sounds. On account of his foul smelling, suppurating wounded foot his companions make the decision to desert him since they cannot bear the smell and they remove him to a nearby island and sail off to Troy without him. Philoctetes then endures years of solitude as a social outcast and wanderer, and is eventually rescued from his plight by the son of Achilles, Neoptolemus who is sent to the island on which he dwells and as part of a mission to bring him back with his bow so the Trojans can be finally defeated.[19] The key lesson of the play, or at least one of its key lessons, has been captured well by Edmund Wilson as follows: "The victim of a malodorous disease which renders him abhorrent to society and periodically degrades him and makes him helpless is also the master of a superhuman art which everybody has to respect and which the normal man feels he needs."[20]

The tale of Philoctetes serves for Nietzsche, or so I interpret his enigmatic aphorism, to capture an essential aspect of the search of the free spirit and its way of life: an outsider to normal society, enduring long periods of agonising solitude, and yet committed to the on-going labour of free-spirited thinking, is the figure

---

[19] For Nietzsche's familiarity and identification with the fate of Philoctetes see his letter to Heinrich von Stein from Sils-Maria and dated September 18, 1884, in Middleton, *Selected Letters of Friedrich Nietzsche*, 231.

[20] See Edmund Wilson, *The Wound and the Bow; Seven Studies in Literature* (New York: Oxford University Press, 1947), 294.

that may eventually be of great benefit to others and to society. The task, however, is not to resolve the problem of existence once and for all but to persist in the search for knowledge, and in so doing resist the temptation of tranquil rest offered by the peaceful and enchanted gardens of Armida.

But what of the garden of Epicurus: does this not offer an idyllic mode of retreat? For Nietzsche the garden of Epicurus does not represent, as might be supposed, a retreat from existence, but is for him a place where one can find the time necessary to undertake the labours of the free spirit. The Epicurean attachment of life entails a specific mode of being in the world, a new attunement to nature as a source of pleasure, removing oneself from the false infinite and stripping away various disabling phantasms such as the idea of immortality with its regime of infinite pleasures and eternal punishments. There remains a strong and firm desire for life but, as Nietzsche points out, this voluptuous appreciation and enjoyment of life is of a modest kind: it is modest in terms of the kinds of pleasure it wants from existence and cultivates, and in terms of its acknowledgment of the realities of a human existence. This is a happiness that Nietzsche appreciates and admires, seeing it as the essential component of the heroic-idyllic mode of philosophizing in which the mind's illusions about the world are stripped away and one is left with a way of being in the world that brings true pleasure since the mind has been liberated from the terrors, superstitions, and phantoms that disturb it. Epicurus is one of the first naturalists since he speaks about nature rather than the gods and wants us to focus our attention on this. This, then, is a philosophy as a project of demystification and a new way of life, with the human being living a modest life. This Epicurean way of life and of being the world is based on a free-spirited search for knowledge, and this might be the reason why even the late Nietzsche, who is critical of Epicurus, can continue to write of an Epicurean "bent for knowledge" that does not easily let go of the questionable character of things (GS 375).

Joy over Pleasure

In the preface to *On the Genealogy of Morality* Nietzsche associates philosophical cheerfulness (*Heiterkeit*) with the gay science and he speaks of this cheerfulness as a reward: "a reward for a long, brave, diligent, subterranean seriousness..." (GM Preface 7)[21] The idea that cheerfulness constitutes a cultivated philosophical disposition is of Democritean and Epicurean ancestry; the idea that it may be a reward for intellectual seriousness is of Epicurean

---

[21] Nietzsche, *On the Genealogy of Morality*, trans. Carol Diethe (Cambridge: Cambridge University Press, 2006).

inspiration. In *De Rerum Natura* Lucretius, the great disciple of Epicurus, address the "joyless hearts of men" (see the opening of book two of the text), and writes of the joyful character of his intellectual labours as a reward, specifically as a "reward for teaching on these lofty topics" and "for struggling to loose men's minds from the tight knots of superstition and shedding on dark material the bright beam of my song…"[22]

Nietzsche is strongly wedded to the rewards of joy over the less intense and more comfortable experiences of pleasure. In the preface to the second edition of *The Gay Science*, composed near Genoa in the autumn of 1886, Nietzsche writes importantly on this topic, seeking to highlight his commitment to a joyful enlightenment as his principal intellectual project. He is not seeking to become a "better" human being, but only a more "profound" one, and this preference is what informs and guides the kind of inquiry undertaken by the gay or joyful science as an enlightenment endeavour:

> The attraction of everything problematic, the delight in an *x*, however, is so great in such more spiritual, more spiritualized men that this delight flares up again and again like a bright blaze over all the distress of what is problematic, over all the danger of uncertainty, and even over the jealousy of the lover. We know a new happiness (GS Preface 3).

The joys of experience, as well as the joys of the gay scientist, are born from privation and abysses, including abysses of sickness; here, however, one returns to life newborn and "with a more delicate taste for joy (*Freude*)" (GS Preface 4). Indeed, Nietzsche writes of "a second dangerous innocence in joy" in which one is now more childlike "and yet a hundred times subtler than one has ever been before" (ibid.). One has returned to life from the abysses of existence not with abjectness or with cynical despair, not with jadedness or unwarranted loftiness, but with this innocence in joy that restores one to childhood – one is full of hope and anticipation – and yet one has acquired all the subtleties of age and maturation. There is clearly an element of surprise in the experience of joy, and this is a dimension Nietzsche captures well in his preface: as sick one was deprived of hope but one is now suddenly attacked by the hope of great health. As a convalescent Nietzsche is surprised by the hopes given to him in his return to health and to life. In his study of the story of joy Adam Potkay notes that in Greek joy (chara) is etymologically connected to grace (charis) and as the gift that

---

22 Lucretius, *On the Nature of the Universe*, book four, lines 6-9.

is freely given. He notes further: "One may feel satisfied or relieved by a success one feels one deserves; one rejoices, however, in what comes as more or less a gift or surprise."[23] Only in the course of the slow and painful maturation of his ideas, of his philosophy, and of the gay science, does Nietzsche come to experience the reward of his intellectual pursuits, and this makes the joyful character of his scientific practice all the sweeter and more delicate.

Nietzsche favours this delicate art of a gay science over the intellectual experiences of pleasure that characterize modernity. Indeed, he tells us in the preface that the "crude, musty, brown pleasure" of the 'educated' (*Gebildeten*) strikes him as repulsive, whilst the sublime of the "romantic uproar" – "elevated, inflated, exaggerated" – hurts his senses, including his sense of hearing (the reference is surely to Wagner's music). Writing as a convalescent – since he has returned from sickness and its abysses – he finds himself in need of an 'art' that is 'mocking, light, fleeting, divinely untroubled' (ibid.). The will to truth that pursues truth at any price is to be viewed as a piece of youthful madness and as bad taste: gay scientists are "too experienced, too serious, too merry, too burned, too *profound*" to have belief in a simple-minded love of truth. Moreover, "Today we consider it a matter of decency not to wish to see everything naked, or to be present at everything, or to understand and 'know' everything" (ibid.).

Nietzsche's fundamental teaching in the preface to the second edition of *The Gay Science* is that without sickness and great pain we cannot be genuine questioners of existence. If we are to become such questioners we need to be shaken out of our familiar and complacent attitude towards life and out of a secure being in the world. However, this questioning out of the abysses of existence and the depths of experience is not to be motivated by despair or disappointment but rather by the rewards of joy, including the joy of anticipation, expectation, and amazement: in short, there are now "new seas" to navigate and explore.

Conclusion

In this short essay I have sought to illuminate aspects of Nietzsche's search for happiness and joy. I have not covered, owing to lack of space, one important contrast and opposition we encounter in the late Nietzsche, namely, that between "Dionysian joy" (*Lust*) and "Epicurean delight" (*Vergnügen*).[24] However, Karl

---

[23] Adam Potkay, *The Story of Joy: From the Bible to Romanticism*, 12.

[24] "I have presented such terrible images to knowledge that any 'Epicurean delight' is out of the question, Only Dionysian joy is sufficient: *I have been the first to discover the tragic*" (KSA 11, 25 [95]; WP 1029).

Jaspers notes that one enters the garden of Epicurus in order, overcoming oneself, to abandon it once again, and this neatly captures something of the character of Nietzsche's attachment to Epicurus in the course of his intellectual development.[25]

In his attachment to pleasure and need to flee from pain with a religion of love Nietzsche comes to see him as a typical decadent (AC 30),[26] and we need to reflect carefully on whether this is an accurate and fair-minded conception of Epicurean way of life. We might see, as Schopenhauer did, the Epicurean quest for *ataraxia* as akin to the Buddhist attainment of Nirvana.[27] This is how one commentator has seen the Epicurean philosophy, entailing the attainment of the highest enjoyment in the removal of all vivid sensations, including pain, desire, and activity.[28] However, the garden of Epicurus is not an idyll that seeks escape from being or that refuses to acknowledge the terrible character of existence. As one commentator on Nietzsche's reception of Epicurus has put it, Epicurus's denial of immortality, "affirms the most terrible character of existence as one of the first principles of the good life."[29] It is even suggested that we find in Epicurus a conception of human existence and the world that is more finite and hence more terrible than Nietzsche's (Epicurus lives without the consolation – if that is what it is - of eternal recurrence). Moreover, Epicurus's remaining true to the earth "was not pathologically conditioned by his desire to put an end to suffering and pain"; rather, it is the case that his "insight into the unity of truth and appearances arose out of a profound recognition of human finitude."[30] In Epicurean *ataraxia* we encounter "the calm of strength and nothing of the calm of weakness."[31] Far from being the repose of the deepest sleep, as the late Nietzsche supposes, such *ataraxia* is "an awakening of the active forces of life, an

---

[25] Karl Jaspers, *The Great Philosophers, volume III*, 111.

[26] Nietzsche, *The Anti-Christ*, trans. Judith Norman (Cambridge: Cambridge University Press, 2005).

[27] For further insight into Nietzsche's "Epicurus" as mediated by Schopenhauer see Fritz Bornmann, "Nietzsches Epikur," *Nietzsche-Studien*, 13 (1984), 177-89; and Andrea Christian Bertino, "Nietzsche und die hellenistische Philosophie: Der Übermensch und der Weise," *Nietzsche-Studien* 36 (2007), 95-131. See also Roos, 2000, 293. Roos also notes the influence of Montaigne and Jacob Burckhardt on Nietzsche's appreciation of Epicurus.

[28] See A. H. J. Knight, "Nietzsche and Epicurean Philosophy," *Philosophy*, 8, 1933, 431-445, 439.

[29] Joseph P. Vincenzo, "Nietzsche and Epicurus," 383-97, 387.

[30] Ibid., 390.

[31] Ibid., 391.

affirmation of the world as an aesthetic outpouring."[32] This is to say that for the Epicurean *ataraxia* "is a direct experience of the intrinsic pleasure of life itself, of the active forces of a life form freed from the reactive force of desire." We now directly participate in the blessed life of the gods, "dwelling in the divine state of forbearance from reaction."[33]

The later evaluation of Epicurus we find in Nietzsche clearly stands in marked contrast to the appreciation we find in his free spirit period. In the middle writings Epicurus is deployed, at least in part, as a way of breaking with fanatical enthusiasms and intoxications, including quite possibly Nietzsche's own early Dionysian ones. The serene teaching of Epicurus provides Nietzsche with one way of shedding his previous skin, that of *The Birth of Tragedy*, and now conducting the patient labour of self-analysis and self-cultivation as a therapy of body and soul. For the middle period Nietzsche Epicurus is the philosopher who affirms the moment, having neither resentment toward the past nor fear of the future.[34] Moreover, he teaches us the value of self-sufficiency and his cultivation of a refined egoism greatly appeals to Nietzsche. Nietzsche finds in Epicurus a victory over pessimism in which death becomes the last celebration of a life that is constantly embellished.[35] This last of the Greek philosophers teaches the joy of living in the midst of a world in decay and where all moral doctrines preach suffering. As Richard Roos puts it, "The example of Epicurus teaches that a life filled with pain and renunciation prepares one to savour the little joys of the everyday better. Relinquishing Dionysian intoxication, Nietzsche becomes a student of this master of moderate pleasures and careful dosages."[36] Like Epicurus, then, Nietzsche seeks to live and philosophize "away from the masses, without masters or gods, idyllically and heroically."[37] Here we encounter that "refined heroism" that accepts death without fear and chooses not to even speak about it. Roos asks what I think is the decisive question concerning this appropriation of Epicurus: can this teaching fill the void left by the loss of faith, the abandonment of Schopenhauer, and the renunciation of Dionysian music? His answer to the question is incisive: "he clings to Epicurus and his consolations with a vigour proportional to the violence of the Christian temptation."[38] In

---

[32] Ibid., 392.

[33] Ibid.

[34] Howard Caygill, "The Consolation of Philosophy; or neither Dionysus nor the Crucified," 131-51, 144.

[35] Richard Roos, "Nietzsche et Épicure: l'idylle héroique," 283-350, 299.

[36] Ibid., 309.

[37] Ibid. 303.

[38] Ibid. 333.

Epicurus Nietzsche discovers what Roos calls aptly an "irresistible power" and a rare strength of spirit, and quotes Nietzsche from 1880: "I found strength in the very places one does not look for it, in simple, gentle and helpful men…powerful natures dominate, that is a necessity, even if those men do not move one finger. And they bury themselves, in their lifetime, in a pavilion in their garden (KSA 9, 6 [206])."[39]

Works Cited

Bett, Richard, "Nietzsche, the Greeks, and Happiness (with special reference to Aristotle and Epicurus)," *Philosophical Topics*, 33: 2, 2005, 45—70, 45.

Caygill, Howard. "The Consolation of Philosophy; or neither Dionysus nor the Crucified," *Journal of Nietzsche Studies*, 7, 1994, 131-51, 144.

Jaspers, Karl. *The Great Philosophers, volume III*, (New York, Harcourt Brace & Company, 1993), 111.

Keazor, Henry. *Poussin* (Köln: Taschen, 2007), p. 57.

Langer, Monika M. *Nietzsche's Gay Science: Dancing Coherence* (Basingstoke: Palgrave Macmillan, 2010), 67.

Lucretius, *On the Nature of the Universe*, trans. R. E. Latham, revised by John Godwin (Middlesex: Penguin, 1994), book four, lines 6-9.

Nietzsche, *Twilight of the Idols*, trans. Duncan Large (Oxford: Oxford University Press, 1998).

—*The Wanderer and His Shadow* in *Human, all too Human*, volume two, trans. Gary Handwerk (Stanford: Stanford University Press, 2013), 295.

—*Dawn: Thoughts on the Presumptions of Morality*, trans. Brittain Smith (Stanford: Stanford University Press, 2011).

—*Human, all too Human*, trans. Gary Handwerk (Stanford: Stanford University Press, 1995).

—*On the Genealogy of Morality*, trans. Carol Diethe (Cambridge: Cambridge University Press, 2006).

—*The Anti-Christ*, trans. Judith Norman (Cambridge: Cambridge University Press, 2005).

Potkay, Adam. *The Story of Joy: From the Bible to Romanticism* (Cambridge University Press, 2007), 12.

---

[39] Ibid. 300.

Roos, Richard. "Nietzsche et Épicure: l'idylle héroique," in Jean-François Balaudé and Patrick Wotling (eds.), *Lectures de Nietzsche* (Paris: Librairie Générale Française, 2000), 283-350, 322.

—"Nietzsche et Épicure: l'idylle héroique," in Jean-François Balaudé and Patrick Wotling (eds.), *Lectures de Nietzsche* (Paris: Librairie Générale Française, 2000), 283-350, 299.

Vincenzo, Joseph P. "Nietzsche and Epicurus," *Man and World*, 27 (1994), 383-97, 387.

Great Politics and the Unnoticed Life:

Nietzsche and Epicurus on the Boundaries of Cultivation

Peter S. Groff

After virtually a century of neglect, Epicurus has in recent years come to be recognized for the significant influence he had on Nietzsche and the central, if ambivalent, place he holds in his thought.[1] Their affinities are many, but two points of intersection in particular deserve mention: a staunch opposition to metaphysico-moralistic interpretations of the world (Laurence Lampert situates them both in the "subterranean tradition" of philosophical naturalism)[2] and an understanding of philosophy as a 'way of life' (*bios*) or 'art of living' (*technē tou biou*).[3] As Keith Ansell-Pearson has pointed out, Epicurus looms largest in

---

[1] While Nietzsche's relationship to Epicurus was sometimes acknowledged in passing, there were until recently relatively few sustained discussions of Nietzsche's view of Epicurus. Some noteworthy exceptions prior to the twenty-first century are A. H. J. Knight, "Nietzsche and Epicurean Philosophy," *Philosophy* Vol. 8, No. 32 (Oct 1933), pp. 431-45; Fritz Bornmann, "Nietzsches Epikur," *Nietzsche Studien*, Band 13 (1984), pp. 177-88; Joseph P. Vincenzo, "Nietzsche and Epicurus," *Man and World* 27, no. 4 (October 1994), pp. 383–397 and Marcin Milkowski, "Idyllic Heroism: Nietzsche's View of Epicurus," *Journal of Nietzsche Studies* 15 (1998), pp. 70–79.

[2] Laurence Lampert, *Nietzsche and Modern Times: A Study of Bacon, Descartes, and Nietzsche* (New Haven & London: Yale University Press, 1993), p. 444. On this affinity, see Howard Caygill, "Under the Epicurean Skies," *Angelaki* 11, no. 3 (December 2006), pp. 107–115; Peter S. Groff, "Leaving the Garden: al-Rāzī and Nietzsche as Wayward Epicureans," *Philosophy East and West* 64:4 (Oct. 2014), 983-1017; and most notably, Keith Ansell-Pearson's recent work (see below).

[3] See e.g., Keith Ansell-Pearson, "True to the Earth: Nietzsche's Epicurean Care of Self and World," in *Nietzsche's Therapeutic Teaching: For Individuals and Culture*, ed. Horst Hutter and Eli Friedland (London: Bloomsbury, 2013), pp. 97–116, "Heroic-Idyllic Philosophizing: Nietzsche and the Epicurean Tradition," *Philosophical Traditions*, ed. Anthony O'Hear, *Royal Institute of Philosophy Supplement* 74 (2014), pp. 237-64, and "'We Are Experiments': Nietzsche on Morality and Authenticity," in *Nietzsche and the Becoming of Life*, ed. Vanessa Lemm (New York: Fordham University Press, 2014), pp. 277–299, and "The Need for Small Doses: Nietzsche, Fanaticism, and Epicureanism," in *Aurore, tournant dans l'œuvre de Nietzsche?* ed. Celine Denat and Patrick Wotling (Reims: ÉPURE, 2015), pp. 193-227. On the recuperation of this ancient model of philosophy as way of life or art of living, see Pierre Hadot, *Philosophy as a Way of Life: Spiritual Exercises from Socrates to Foucault*, ed. and intro. Arnold I. Davidson, trans. Michael Chase (Oxford: Blackwell, 1995), and *What is Ancient Philosophy?* trans. Michael Chase (Cambridge:

Nietzsche middle period works, where select aspects of his thought and life are valorized and appropriated: his vitality, modesty, "heroic-idyllic" mode of philosophizing, therapeutic technique of multiple explanations, embrace of a deathbound soul and rejection of an afterlife, pre-emptive war on Christianity and anticipation of a modern scientific, de-deified worldview.[4] This paper focuses on one aspect of Epicurus' teachings that has as yet received little attention: his controversial advice to "live unnoticed" (*lathe biōsas*).[5] Nietzsche was familiar with this credo and took it to heart, but it ultimately stood at odds with, and lost out to, his irresistible temptation to engage in great politics. The following discussion is an attempt to track Nietzsche's conflicted appreciation for the virtues of the unnoticed life.

Harvard University Press, 2002). See also Michel Foucault, *The Care of the Self*, trans. Robert Hurley (New York: Random House, 1986) and *Technologies of the Self: A Seminar with Michel Foucault*, ed. Luther H. Martin et al. (Amherst: University of Massachusetts Press, 1988), Martha Nussbaum, *The Therapy of Desire: Theory and Practice in Hellenistic Ethics* (Princeton: Princeton University Press, 1994), and Alexander Nehamas' *The Art of Living: Socratic Reflections from Plato to Foucault* (Berkeley: University of California Press, 1998).

[4] On the continuing vitality of Epicurus' thought, see AOM 48 and WS 227; on his modesty, see WS 192 and GS 45; on his greatness and heroic-idyllic mode of philosophizing see WS 295 and WS 332, as well as Ansell-Pearson, "Heroic-Idyllic Philosophizing" and Milkowski, "Idyllic Heroism"; on his higher cultural-spiritual status compared to other Hellenistic philosophers, see HH 275 and GS 306; on his therapeutic technique of multiple explanations (*pleonachos tropos*) see WS 7 and GS 375, as well as Wilson H. Shearin, "Misunderstanding Epicurus? A Nietzschean Identification," *Journal of Nietzsche Studies* 45.1 (Spring 2014), pp. 68-83; on his embrace of a deathbound soul and rejection of an afterlife see D 72 and Z P, 6, as well as Morgan Rempel "Daybreak 72: Nietzsche, Epicurus and the After Death," *Journal of Nietzsche Studies* 43.2 (Autumn 2012), pp. 49-68; on his pre-emptive war on Christianity, see A 58 and KSA 13:16[15]; on his anticipation of a modern scientific, de-deified worldview, see HH 68 and Groff, "Leaving the Garden"; for an Epicurean anticipation of the death of God, see WS 84. Nietzsche's later writings take an increasingly unsympathetic view Epicurus, specifically his atomistic materialism (GS 109, 373, BGE 12, TI, "Reason," 5), his hedonism (BGE 225), and his sickness and decadence (BT P4, GS P2 and 370, GM III.6 and 17, TI "Morality," 3, A 30, KSA 11:25[95]).

[5] Herman Usener, *Epicurea* (Cambridge: Cambridge University Press, 2010), Fragment 551. For the most comprehensive discussion of the *lathe biōsas* teaching, see Geert Roskam, *'Live Unnoticed': On the Vicissitudes of an Epicurean Doctrine* (Leiden: Brill, 2007). *Lathe* has been rendered variously as "hidden," "inconspicuously," "in obscurity," "unobtrusively," "secretly," etc.

A Buried Epicurean Teaching

As traditionally interpreted, the *lathe biōsas* doctrine counsels us to avoid the political life and opt instead for a quiet, sequestered life of contemplation. Most of what we know about it comes to us through doxographies and later critics of Epicurus, but one can nevertheless find similar sentiments scattered throughout the extant remains of his corpus.[6] For instance, he repeatedly warns against the limits of attaining security through other human beings (*asphaleia ex anthrōpōn*).[7] He urges his adherents not to seek happiness in fame or honor and to shun the multitude.[8] He contends that "the purest security is that which comes from a quiet life and withdrawal from the many."[9] Elsewhere, he encourages his followers to "free themselves from the prison of daily duties and politics" and not to get involved with the political life (*me politeuesthai*).[10]

Unsurprisingly, Epicurus' doctrine of the hidden life was wildly unpopular in its time and has remained so to this day. It ran against the grain not only of common opinion (which placed great emphasis on traditional civic values, as well as reputation, honor, and fame), but also against the views of most philosophers. Socrates himself admittedly eschewed political offices, but nonetheless provided an even greater public service though his zetetic activities in the marketplace—ultimately, at the cost of his own life. Plato, envisioning the ideal coincidence of political power and wisdom in the wake of Socrates' death, placed philosophers at the very center of the city as its rulers.[11] For Aristotle, the human being is the *zōon politikon*: human flourishing is simply impossible shorn of certain political advantages and perks, and even the optimal life of contemplation seems to require recognition and acknowledgment—an intellectual fame of sorts—from a community of expert knowers. And the Stoics, despite their famous withdrawal

---

[6] As Roskam points out, "One of the sad consequences of the manuscript tradition of Epicurus' works is the that the maxim *lathe biōsas* has in the end applied its own advice. For indeed, it nowhere appears in the extant writings of Epicurus, leading, as it were, to its own hidden life, far away from inquisitive or boring scholars" (33).

[7] *Principle Doctrines* 6 and 7 (henceforth PD).

[8] *Vatican Sentences* 64 (cf. PD 7) and 81 (henceforth VS).

[9] PD 14. All translations from *The Epicurus Reader*, trans and ed. Brad Inwood and L. P. Gerson (Indianapolis: Hackett, 1994). Cf. Usener, fragment 187.

[10] VS 58 and Diogenes Laertius 10.119 (henceforth DL); cf. DL 10.10: "So gentlemanly was [Epicurus] that he did not even participate in political life.".

[11] He also contrived to mold existing rulers into something resembling a philosopher king, e.g., his ill-fated engagement with Dionysius II—which led Epicurus mockingly to describe Plato as "golden" (*chrusoun*) and his followers as "flatters of Dionysius" (*Dionysiokolakes*) i.e., tyrants' sycophants. See DL 10.8; cf. BGE 7.

into the 'inner citadel', nonetheless acknowledged the duties we have to our communities as rational and virtuous beings, and so saw an ethical obligation to take part in politics.

Epicurus' unapologetically apolitical stance represents such a striking divergence from the norm that it is sometimes explained away in historicist or psychologistic terms, e.g., as a function of the political malaise following Alexander the Great (the retreat from the polis to the individual), or a shortcoming of his character (excessive gentleness, softness, etc), or perhaps some pivotal traumatic episode that soured him on politics once and for all. But bearing in mind the comparably heretical status of Epicurus' other teachings within the tradition, there's no reason to assume that his rejection of the political requires an ad hoc explanation. As Geert Roskam has argued, it is nothing more nor less than a reasoned philosophical teaching proceeding from his fundamental commitment to pleasure as the highest good. Specifically, Roskam links it to three components of Epicurus' ethical thought: (1) his therapeutic attempt to cure the soul of painful irrational fears and vain desires, (2) his analysis of desire (and consequent recognition that the desires for fame, honor, power, influence, or even to contribute to the public good are neither natural nor necessary), and (3) his prudential calculus of pleasure.[12] Put simply, if one seeks tranquility of the soul (*ataraxia*) and wishes to minimize mental anxiety, a private life off the radar is far preferable to a public, political one. But if the human being is for Epicurus not necessarily a political animal, we nonetheless require some degree of sociality to lead good lives. Hence Epicurus' Garden: a small, relatively independent community of friends hidden away from the city and its empty distractions, engaged in revivifying philosophical therapy, cultivating themselves into god-like beings who live lives of quite, simple, stable, tranquil pleasure in accordance with the "deep-set boundary stone" of nature.[13] To understand the radical significance of the Garden for the philosophical life, it is necessary to place it against the background of Epicurus' canonical antipode Plato, and his own attempt to resolve the tension between philosophy and the city. As suggested above, Plato attempts, in the *Republic* at least, to accomplish this by dragging the philosophers from the margins of the *polis* to its very center as rulers. But as Socrates and his

---

[12] Roskam, pp. 34-35.
[13] Cf. DL 10.121b: "[The sage] will found a school, but not so as to draw a crowd." On the "deep-set boundary stone" (*alte terminus haerens*), which indicates the necessary limitations of nature according to which we should think and live (and thus rules out vain fears and desires), see Lucretius, *On the Nature of Things* I.77, cf. I.596, II.1087, III.787, 794, 990, and 1014.

comrades construct their "Fine and Noble City" in speech, an even more beautiful counter-image repeatedly presents itself to them: the ancient dream of the "Blessed Isles," where philosophers can dwell in contemplative peace apart from the wearisome, soul-grinding business of the state.[14] The best Socrates can do, though, is to dangle this primordial utopia in front of the philosopher-guardians as a vague promissory note while they grudgingly discharge their political duties. Epicurus' Garden is in effect the ancient dream of the Blessed Isles made concrete, in the here and now.[15]

Great Politics and the Platonic Philosopher-Legislator

There is an obvious sense in which Nietzsche can be said to share Epicurus' dismissive views on the political. For instance, he repeatedly distances himself from the interests of the state even in his early writings: "he who has the *furor philosophicus* within him," he writes, "will already no longer have time for the *furor politicus* and will wisely refrain from reading the newspapers every day, let alone working for a political party" (SE 7, p. 181).[16] And Nietzsche is forever reminding

---

[14] The Blessed Isles (*makarōn nesoi*) are in Greek myth an eschatological paradise located in the far Western streams of Okeanos where the elite few – originally heroes, later the righteous, in Platonic dialogues, philosophers—live eternally and happily. They begin as a conception of the afterlife (in opposition to Hades; later merged with Elysium), but in some versions become merely a place where life is easiest and best for mortals on earth. In the *Republic*, they become a kind of sop thrown to the philosopher-rulers: Socrates promises that after they have discharged their civic duty, they will be allowed to return to their contemplative life, this time on the Isles of the Blessed, while new guardians take over and pay back their own debt to the city (*Republic* 540b). Whether the philosophers ever finally liberate themselves from the tyranny of the city hinges on whether we understand this concession as the prospect of a happy retirement or simply a blithe recognition of their eventual death. An earlier remark made by Socrates (*Republic* 519c) would suggest that they function as at most a kind of afterworldly reward. For other references to the Blessed Isles in Plato's dialogues, see *Symposium* 179e, 180b and *Gorgias* 523b, 524a. For pre-Platonic sources, see Hesiod, *Works and Days*, 167-173, Pindar, *Olympian Odes*, 2.68-80, and Herodotus, *Histories*, 3.26.1. See Eckart Olshausen, "Makarōn Nesoi" and Christine Sourvinou Inwood, "Elysium," in *Brill's New Pauly Encyclopedia of the Ancient World: Antiquity* (Leiden: E. J. Brill 2006).

[15] On this, see Bernard Frischer, *The Sculpted Word: Epicureanism and Philosophical Recruitment in Ancient Greece* (Berkeley: University of California, 1982), p. 38.

[16] I use Walter Kaufmann's translations for Penguin/Vintage and R.J. Hollingdale's translations for Cambridge University Press, with occasional emendations in favor of greater literalness. The single exception is Graham Parkes' recent translation of *Thus Spoke Zarathustra* for Oxford. Translations of passages from the *Nachlass* or letters are my own unless otherwise noted. Cf. SE 6, p. 165, where he defends a conception of

us of his disdain for the petty nationalistic politics of Bismarck's *Reich*, pointing out that the growth of political and military power inevitably comes at the cost of cultural degeneration and "spiritual flattening" (*geistige Verflachung*).[17] In these respects, Nietzsche can perhaps fairly describe himself as "the last *antipolitical* German" (EH "Wise," 3).[18] Of course, being *antipolitisch* is not the same as being *unpolitisch*—apolitical, indifferent to politics—an attitude that arguably aligns more closely with Epicurus' maxim. Put differently, the relevant choice for Nietzsche is not between politics or no politics, but between small politics (*kleine Politik*) and great politics (*grosse Politik*).[19] Politics becomes great when an actual "revaluation of all values" is at stake, when it involves a cultural "war of spirits"

---

education (*Bildung*) "that makes one a solitary, that proposes goals that transcend money and money-making, that takes a long time," characterizing it (affirmatively, in spite of popular opinion) as "'refined egoism' and 'immoral cultural Epicureanism'."

[17] See e.g. TI, "Germans," *passim*; cf. BGE 241.

[18] On this, see Peter Bergmann, *Nietzsche, "The Last Antipolitical German"* (Bloomington, IN: Indian University Press, 1987). I set aside here the deeper and more difficult question whether Nietzsche does have a political philosophy in any traditional sense, and if so, how it ought to be understood. The literature on this question is steadily growing and far too voluminous to cite comprehensively, but see e.g. Tracy Strong, *Nietzsche and Politics of Transfiguration* (Urbana, IL: University of Illinois, 1975/2000), Keith Ansell-Pearson, *An Introduction to Nietzsche as Political Thinker* (Cambridge: Cambridge University Press, 1994), Lawrence J. Hatab, *A Nietzschean Defense of Democracy* (Chicago and La Salle, IL: Open Court, 1995), Daniel W. Conway, *Nietzsche and the Political* (London: Routledge, 1997), Frederick Appel, *Nietzsche Contra Democracy* (Ithaca, NY: Cornell University Press, 1999), and Tamsin Shaw, *Nietzsche's Political Skepticism* (Princeton: Princeton University Press, 2010), as well as three excellent recent anthologies: *Nietzsche, Power and Politics: Rethinking Nietzsche's Legacy for Political Thought*, ed. Herman W. Siemens and Vasti Roodt (Berlin: Walter de Gruyter, 2008), *Nietzsche and Political Thought*, ed. Keith Ansell-Pearson (New York: Bloomsbury, 2013), and *Nietzsche as Political Philosopher*, eds. Manuel Knoll and Barry Stocker (Berlin: Walter de Gruyter, 2014).

[19] Nietzsche's use of the the expression *grosse Politik* is sparse and not exactly univocal. Sometimes it's loosely associated with any agent—princes, rulers, masses—that is spurred by the need for the feeling of power (D 189); sometimes it's used ironically and in scare quotes to describe the shallow, petty, provincial power politics of the *Reich* (BGE 241, 254); sometimes it has to do with the "the struggle for the dominion of the world," which at first may seem to indicate simply a more ambitious transnational European or world political power conflict (BGE 208). His final usage of it, however, suggests that it ultimately signifies a spiritual-cultural struggle for the future of the human (EH, "Destiny," 1).

(*Geisterkrieg*) rather than merely a crude power conflict over legal systems, economic policies, material resources or national boundaries (EH, "Destiny," 1).

"It is only with me," Nietzsche famously claims, "that the earth knows *great politics*" (ibid.). An immodest, self-mythologizing claim perhaps, since elsewhere he recognizes that initiating such world-transforming revaluations is precisely the true task of the *philosopher*:

> Genuine philosophers, however, are commanders and legislators [*Befehlende und Gesetzgeber*]: they say, "*thus* it *shall* be!" They first determine the Whither and For What of humankind . . . With a creative hand they reach for the future and all that is and has been becomes a means for them, an instrument, a hammer. Their "knowing" is *creating*, their creating is a legislation, their will to truth is—*will to power*. (BGE 211)[20]

Interestingly, in the *Nachlass* drafts for this passage from 1884-85, Nietzsche even points to Plato and Muhammad as paradigmatic examples of commanders and legislators, despite the residual self-deception under which they were laboring. That is to say, Nietzsche sees these predecessors as involved in the same sort of transformative world-historical task that he himself is qua philosopher; they are simply less self-aware of the radically creative nature of their legislations.[21] And indeed, it seems particularly appropriate for Nietzsche to place himself in the lineage of Plato here, since the conception of philosophers as "commanders and legislators"—even *prophets* in the manner of Zarathustra—is itself a distinctly Platonic idea. Nietzsche's nomothetic great politics can thus be understood as a late modern radicalization of Platonic political philosophy: specifically, the ideal coincidence of wisdom and political power epitomized by the philosopher-king.[22]

---

[20] Nietzsche grants this privileged status to the philosopher even in his early writings. See e.g. SE 3, p. 144; cf. Z III, "On Old and New Tablets," 2.

[21] There are of course other differences too: their teachings are afterworldly, ostensibly universal, transcultural and ahistorical, etc.

[22] On Nietzsche as Platonic political philosopher, see Leo Strauss, "Note on the Plan of Nietzsche's *Beyond Good and Evil*," in *Studies in Platonic Political Philosophy* (Chicago: University of Chicago Press, 1983), pp. 174-191, Stanley Rosen, *The Mask of Enlightenment: Nietzsche's Zarathustra* (Cambridge: Cambridge Unity Press, 1995), Laurence Lampert, *Nietzsche and Modern Times: A Study of Bacon, Descartes and Nietzsche* (New Haven, CT: Yale University Press, 1993), *Leo Strauss and Nietzsche* (Chicago: University of Chicago, 1997), and *Nietzsche's Task: An Interpretation of Beyond Good and Evil* (New Haven, CT: Yale University Press, 2001), Horst Hutter, *Shaping the Future: Nietzsche's New Regime of the Soul and Its Ascetic Practices* (Lanham, MD: Lexington Books, 2005) and Groff, "Wisdom and Violence," pp. 71-75.

His new philosophical legislators, however, do not pretend to transmit some preexistent universal Good to us, nor are they trying simply to realign the human soul with the rational and moral order of things; rather, they are bringing into being a new table of goods according to which humanity can live, and in doing so are experimentally attempting to transform humanity. They must accordingly prepare "great ventures and over-all attempts of discipline and cultivation [*Zucht und Züchtung*]" in order to determine the future of the human (BGE 203). This ambitious project of transfiguration is crystalized in the dramatic image of Zarathustra attempting to produce his *Übermensch* from the ugly, uncarved stone of humanity (Z II, "Upon the Isles of the Blessed").[23]

Concealment and the Discreet Therapeutic Philosopher

Yet Platonic as this all sounds, one can nevertheless find deeper Epicurean reservations in Nietzsche's thought even here. For the Nietzschean philosopher-lawgiver is a shadowy, unobtrusive, hidden figure who dwells far from the centers of conventional political power, shunning fame and the recognition of the masses.[24] As Zarathustra says in his initial condemnation of the city: "Around inventors of new values the world revolves—invisibly [*unsichtbar*] it revolves. Yet around play-actors the people and fame revolve: that is 'the way of the world'" (Z I, "On the Flies of the Marketplace"). This same line is repeated later on after he and his students have abandoned the city, albeit with a small alteration: "Not around the inventors of new noise," he says, "but around the inventors of new values does the world revolve, *inaudibly* [*unhörbar*] it revolves." (Z II, "On Great Events").[25] A powerful but confusing image: what would it mean for the world

---

[23] See BGE 62 and 225 for similar sculptural metaphors. Cf. Z III, "On Old and New Tablets," 29: "And blessedness it must seem to you to press your hand upon millennia as upon wax . . ."

[24] A beautiful aphorism from *Daybreak* entitled "*Do not perish unnoticed,*" (D 435) would at first seem to suggestive an explicit repudiation of Epicurus' teaching, insofar as his counsel to live unnoticed was often understood as entailing that we should die unnoticed (*lathe apobiōsas*). However, D 435 has more to do with the ways in which we gradually get ground down to nothing by the seemingly small, everyday, repetitive details of our lives about which we are inadequately cognizant. In this sense it should be understood against the background of passages like WS 5-6, 16, D 553, and EH, "Clever," 10—Epicurean passages which emphasize the importance of attending to the "closest," "smallest and most everyday things," e.g. diet, housing, clothing, nutrition, place, climate, recreation, etc.

[25] Cf. Z II, "The Stillest Hour": "It is the stillest [*stillsten*] words that bring on the storm. Thoughts that come on dove's feet guide the world."

PETER S. GROFF

to revolve "invisibly" or "inaudibly" around something or someone? It's difficult to envision. The sense seems rather to be that it is the inventors of new values who themselves remain invisible or inaudible to the world, even as they shape it. Certainly Nietzsche saw himself that way as he wandered anonymously throughout southern Europe, and despite his occasional frustrated desire for recognition, believed—in a residually Epicurean spirit—that it was probably for the best.[26] Indeed, Nietzsche's early retirement from the academy in 1879 and the inconspicuous, nomadic regimen that shaped the next ten years of his life were prompted not only by chronic health issues, but by his growing Epicurean inclination to free himself from the prison of daily duties and politics and become a genuine philosopher.[27] It is perhaps not entirely coincidental that his withdrawal from that world left him literally stateless.[28]

As mentioned earlier, it is in Nietzsche's middle period works (1878-1882) that one finds the richest trove of Epicurean insights, and the siren call of the sequestered life is no exception. In describing the "prudence" of free spirits Nietzsche observes,

> [They] will easily be content with, for example, a minor office or an income that just enables them to live; for they will organize their life in such a way that a great transformation of external circumstances, even an overturning of the political order, does not overturn their life with it. Upon all these things they expend as little energy as possible. . . . There is in [the free spirit's] way of living and thinking a *refined heroism* which disdains to offer itself to the veneration of the great masses, as his coarser brother does, and tends to go silently [*still*]

[26] See letters to Heinrich Köselitz, Aug. 26, 1883 (KSB 6, 436) and Dec 10, 1885 (KSB 7, 121-22).
[27] On this, see Paolo D'Iorio, *Nietzsche's Journey to Sorrento: Genesis of the Philosophy of the Free Spirit*, tr. Sylvia Mae Gorelick (Chicago: University of Chicago Press, 2016). Ostensibly an account of Nietzsche's initial voyage to Sorrento during his year of sick leave to live in a friendship community with Malwida von Meysenbug, Paul Rée and Albert Brenner, it provides a rich and insightful portrait of the turn in Nietzsche's life from disenchanted university professor to nomadic philosopher. His middle period works—especially *Human, All Too Human*—are strewn with warnings against the petty, obsessive *vita activa* of modern life; see e.g. HH 283: "As at all times, so too now, human beings are divided into the slaves and the free: for he who does not have two-thirds of his day to himself is a slave, no matter what else he may be: statesman, business, official, scholar."
[28] As D'Iorio points out, due to an unusual combination of circumstances, Nietzsche was by this time no longer a citizen of any country—an appropriate status for a self-proclaimed "good European" (D'Iorio, p. 9).

through the world and out of the world. Whatever labyrinths he may stray through, among whatever rocks his stream may make its torturous way—if he emerges into the open air he will travel his road bright, light and almost soundlessly [*geräuschlos*] and let sunshine play down into his very depths. (HH 291)

The mood and language of this passage is deeply Epicurean: the emphasis on prudence (*Vorsicht*, a common German rendering of *phronēsis*, which is for Epicurus the root of all other virtues), the desideratum of minimizing interaction with and dependency upon the city, the strategy of creating stabilizing bulwarks against social and political disruption, the evocation of refined heroism,[29] the avoidance of the masses, going silently-soundlessly through and out of the world (*lathe biōsas, lathe apobiōsas*), and the themes of open air and sunlight.[30] But who is the "coarser brother" (*gröberer Bruder*) of this Epicurean free spirit who seeks popular veneration? The meddling Socratic gadfly? The Platonic philosopher ruler? The vain Peripatetic seeking recognition as a knower? More likely, it is either the theatrical Cynic- or the Stoic-type, both of whom Nietzsche elsewhere compares unfavorably to the more nuanced, cultural and spiritual Epicurean.[31]

---

[29] Cf. SE 6, p. 165 and WS 295. On Nietzsche's appropriation of Epicurus' "refined egoism" as a kind of naturalistic care of the self, see Ansell-Pearson, "True to the Earth," pp. 97-116; for an excellent discussion of Epicurus as exemplifying the "heroic-idyllic mode of philosophizing," see Ansell-Pearson, "Heroic-Idyllic Philosophizing," pp. 237-63. See also Marcin Milkowski, "Idyllic Heroism: Nietzsche's View of Epicurus," *Journal of Nietzsche Studies* 15 (1998), pp. 70–79.

[30] Nietzsche often associates Epicurus with sunlight (specifically a clear, bright exterior light); see e.g. WS 295, WS 332 and GS 45. Cf. implicitly Epicurean passages where Nietzsche describes his own predilections, e.g. D 553.

[31] See GS 306, which purports to compare the Stoic and the Epicurean as types. The passage has an inescapably autobiographical or even confessional tone: "The Epicurean selects the situation, the persons, and even the events that suit his extremely irritable, intellectual constitution; he gives up all others, which means almost everything, because they would be too strong and heavy for him to digest. . . the Epicurean would rather dispense with [the Stoic's theatrical cultivation to insensitivity], having his 'garden'! For those with whom fate attempts improvisations—those who live in violent ages and and depend on sudden and mercurial people—Stoicism may indeed be advisable. But anyone foresees more or less that fate permits him to spin a long thread does well to make Epicurean arrangements. That is what all those have always done whose work is of the spirit." (GS 306). CF. HH 275, where the Epicurean type is favored over the more ham-fisted Cynic.

One finds reminders of this Epicurean prudence even in the post-Zarathustran works. In *Beyond Good and Evil*, for example, he counsels his nascent free spirits in similar terms:

> Take care, philosophers and friends, of knowledge, and beware of martyrdom! Of suffering "for the truth's sake" [in the manner of Socrates, Spinoza, Giordano Bruno, etc]! . . . Rather, go away. Flee into concealment [*Verborgene*]. And have your masks and your subtlety, that you may be mistaken for what you are not, or feared a little. And don't forget the garden, the garden with golden trelliswork. And have people around you who are as a garden . . . choose the *good* solitude, the free, playful, light solitude that gives you too the right to remain good in some sense. (BGE 25)

Apart from the obvious Epicurean tropes of withdrawal and concealment—earlier in the same book, he describes Epicurus as "hidden away [*versteckt sass*] in his little garden" (BGE 7)—it should be noted that the figure of Epicurus is sometimes associated in Nietzsche's writings with having an unknown or obscured identity: being mistaken for what one is not.[32] And note that even the emphasis on solitude here—an ascetic practice that looms large throughout Nietzsche's corpus—is construed in Epicurean terms: the "good" and "light" solitude is the garden, where one is not entirely alone and never lonely, because there are always healing friends and kindred spirits.[33]

Sometimes this Epicurean withdrawal-concealment strategy is cast as a necessary prologue to more ambitious cultural or even political projects: a desire to be useful on a grander scale. In an aphorism entitled "*The buried*" (*Vergrabenen*), he writes,

[32] On Epicurus' mistaken identity, see WS 227, GS 45 and BGE 7; cf. Letter to Heinrich Köselitz, Aug. 3, 1883 (KSB 6, 418).
[33] On solitude in Nietzsche, see Peter H. Van Ness, "Nietzsche on Solitude: The Spiritual Discipline of the Godless," *Philosophy Today* 32.4 (Winter 1988), pp. 346-358 and Hutter, pp. 47-74. As D'Iorio points out (*Nietzsche's Journey*, p. 16), the original projected title for *Human, All Too Human* was "The Light Life" (*Das leichte Leben*). The initial sketches from 1876 are again strikingly Epicurean in spirit, describing an "art of living" (*Lebenskunst*) that aims not at lightening life (i.e., making it easy for us), and certainly not at making it even harder (so as to offer afterwards some supreme soteriological recipe), but rather helping us "to take life lightly," like the gods, standing before the truth in vivid rapture. See KSA 8:16[7], 17[74] and 17[85].

> We withdraw [*zurückziehen*] into concealment [*Verborgene*]: but not out of any kind of personal ill-humor, as though the political and social situation of the present day were not good enough for us, but because through our withdrawal we want to economize and assemble forces of which culture will *later* have great need, and more so if this present remains *this* present and as such fulfils *its* task. We are accumulating capital and seeking to make it secure: but, as in times of great peril, to do that we have to *bury* it. (WS 229)[34]

The predominant emphasis in the middle period writings, however, is on a more modest task: cooperative therapy and pluralistic experiments in self-cultivation among a small elite circle of like-minded free spirits.[35] This is often juxtaposed with the imprudent desire (rooted in sympathy or pity) to eliminate danger and suffering from the lives of others. An aphorism in *Daybreak* concludes:

> the question itself remains unanswered whether one is of *more use* to another by immediately leaping to his side and *helping* him – which can in any case be only superficial where it does not become a tyrannical seizing and transforming – or by *creating* something out of oneself that the other can behold with pleasure: a beautiful, restful, self-enclosed [*abgeschlossenen*] garden perhaps, with high walls against storms and the dust of the roadway but also a hospitable gate. (D 174)[36]

---

[34] Cf. HH 285, which casts the Epicurean need for contemplative repose (*Ruhe*) in comparable terms. Zarathustra's multiple withdrawals into solitude, away from both the cities and his own disciples, are framed in this way as well. On the notion of a provisional, strategic withdrawal into Epicurean friendship communities in order later to engage in great politics, see Hutter, p. 5.

[35] On this see Graham Parkes, *Composing the Soul: Reaches of Nietzsche's Psychology* (Chicago, University of Chicago, 1994), esp. pp. 157-203, Michael Ure, *Nietzsche's Therapy: Self-Cultivation in the Middle Works* (Lanham: Lexington Books, 2008), and of course, Ansell-Pearson's many article and chapters on Nietzsche and Epicurus.

[36] Cf BGE 25, where one's friends are the garden in a "*good* solitude"; here one becomes the healing, inspiring garden for other like-minded spirits. See also D 194, which similarly contends that instead of offering moral prescriptions for everyone, "One should seek out limited circles and seek to promote morality for them . . . Great success, however, is reserved above all to him who wants educate, not everybody or even limited circles, but a single individual . . . ." This more modest, conservative, selective approach to transfiguration can be seen in other passages from *Daybreak*, e.g., D 534, where he emphasizes "small doses" rather than great revolutions, or D 462, where he advocates "slow cures" of the soul, focusing again on the overlooked "little" things (cf. WS 5-6, 16, D 435, 553). On this theme, see Ansell-Pearson, "The Need for Small Doses."

Interestingly, the Platonic strategy of "tyrannical seizing and transforming" is considered here, but quickly passed over in favor of a more voluntary, private Epicurean cultivation. A year later in *The Gay Science* Nietzsche returns to this idea and unpacks it more carefully. Pointing out the ways in which the causes and inner logic of a person's suffering are for the most part inaccessible or incomprehensible to others—and thus why pity is an ineffective and even counter-productive response to suffering—he encourages philosophical therapists to prioritize their own self-discovery and cultivation and then, by extension, focus only on kindred souls who they can genuinely understand and help. The primary concern is never to lose "one's own way":

> How is it possible to keep to one's own way? Constantly, some clamor or other calls us aside; rarely does our eye behold anything that does not require us to drop our own preoccupation instantly to help. I know, there are a hundred decent and praiseworthy ways of losing *my own way*, and they are truly highly "moral"! Indeed, those who now preach the morality of pity even take the view that precisely this and only this is moral—to lose one's *own* way in order to come to the assistance of a neighbor. I know just as certainly that I only need to expose myself to the sight of some genuine distress and I am lost. And if a suffering friend said to me, "Look, I am about to die; please promise to die with me," I should promise it; and the sight of a small mountain tribe fighting for its liberty would persuade me to offer it my hand and my life . . . All such arousing of pity and calling for help is secretly seductive, for our "own way" is too hard and demanding and too remote from the love and gratitude of others, and we do not really mind escaping from it . . . while I shall keep silent [*verschweigen*, i.e., hide, conceal, keep secret] about some points, I do not want to remain silent about my morality which says to me: Live in seclusion [*Lebe im Verborgenen*, i.e, live secretly, discreetly, in hiding or concealment] so that you *can* live for yourself. Live in *ignorance* about what seems most important to your age. Between yourself and today lay the skin of at least three centuries. And the clamor of today, the noise of wars and revolutions should be a mere murmur for you. You will also wish to help – but only those whose distress you *understand* entirely because they share with you one suffering and one hope – your friends – and only in the manner in which you help yourself. (GS 338)[37]

---

[37] Cf. SE 1, *passim* on the theme of not losing oneself.

The conclusion to this passage ("live in concealment so that you can live for yourself") is an elegant summation of the *lathe biōsas* maxim, and more generally of the kind of refined egoism that drew Nietzsche to Epicurus.

Even when the theme of philosophical *therapeia* is expressed in a more generous, expansive and inclusive mood, the Epicurean watchwords remain. In one such passage, Nietzsche speaks of the desire to "give away one's spiritual house and possessions" in assisting those working on themselves.[38] Such a therapist, Nietzsche suggests,

> is not merely not looking for fame: he would even like to escape gratitude, for gratitude is too importunate and lacks respect for solitude [*Einsamkeit*] and silence [*Stillschweigen*]. What he seeks is to live nameless [*namenlos*] and lightly mocked at, too humble to awaken envy or hostility . . . To be like a little inn which rejects no one who is in need but which is afterwards forgotten or ridiculed! . . . Forever in a kind of love and self-enjoyment! To be in possession of a dominion and at the same time concealed [*verborgen*] and renouncing! To lie continually in the sunshine and gentleness of grace, and yet to know that the paths that rise up to the sublime are close by—That would be a life! That would be a reason for a long life! (D 449)

The emphasis on (relative) solitude, namelessness, silence and concealment is obviously Epicurean, as is the indirect utility of refined egoism, the sunshine motif, the reference to the sublime, and even the evocation of a long life.[39] But in a *Nachlass* note from Autumn 1880, we find a link that tethers this passage even more closely to Epicurus. There he offers a strikingly resonant portrait of the type sketched out above: those who are in possession of a dominion and at the same time concealed and renouncing. "I found strength," he writes, "in the very places one does not look for it, in simple, gentle and helpful human beings, without the slightest inclination to rule. . . powerful natures *dominate*, that is a necessity, even if they do not move one finger. And when they bury [*vergraben*] themselves, in

---

[38] Cf. Z I, "On the Bestowing Virtue."

[39] On the Epicurean compatibility between self-realization and helping select others, see D 174 and GS 338, as well as Keith Ansell-Pearson, "Beyond Selfishness: Epicurean Ethics in Nietzsche and Guyau," in *Nietzsche's Free Spirit Philosophy*, ed. Rebecca Bamford (New York: Rowman and Littlefield, 2015), pp. 49-68; on sunshine as an Epicurean symbol, see again WS 295, WS 332 and GS 45; on Epicurus and the sublime, see WS 295; on the association of Epicureanism and a long life, see GS 306.

their lifetime, in a garden house [*Gartenhaus*]!" (KSA 9:6[206]).[40] Once again, one feels the magnetism of the hidden Epicurus, and with it, Nietzsche's desire to play a similar role.

The Hidden, Helpful Life

To engage with Nietzsche's writings as though he's offering a series of claims that might be true or false is to lose the power of philosophy as a way of life and indeed, to overlook the importance of philosophers as interlocutors, educators and examples.[41] It is tempting, when observing Nietzsche's post-Zarathustran descent into great politics, to conclude that he somehow lost his way—that he should have stuck with his Epicurean experiments in private self-cultivation and not worried about redeeming humanity—but what ultimately is the point of such criticisms? Nietzsche made the moves he made and there's no sense in pronouncing upon what he should have said. But that doesn't mean we have to give up what Nietzsche himself abandoned. Nietzsche took what he wanted from the Greeks in the construction of his own art of living, and we in turn can take what we want from him.[42] Some of it will be useful to us, some of it not. I am of the opinion that his middle period experiments, when he was closest in spirit to Epicurus, are the ones we can profit from the most.[43] Nietzsche is most helpful when he wants least to be noticed, when he is discreet and modest like the powerful philosopher-therapist hidden in the garden: "in possession of a dominion," as he says, "and at the same time concealed and renouncing" (D 449, cf. KSA 9:6[206]). This is the Nietzsche who is the true educator, who liberates and invigorates and augments the lives of his readers. George Eliot, that other great modern Epicurean, perhaps put it best when she observed that

> The growing good of the world is partly dependent on unhistoric acts; and that things are not so ill with you and me as they might have been is half owing to the number who lived faithfully a hidden life, and rest in unvisited tombs.[44]

---

[40] On Epicurus' "powerful nature," see Letter to Heinrich Köselitz, July 1, 1883 (KSB 6, 389); cf. Letter to Heinrich Köselitz, Jan. 22, 1879 (KSB 5, 383). On the image of being "buried" and "concealed" in an Epicurean sense, see WS 229; cf. D 449 and BGE 25.
[41] On this, see SE 1, p. 129-30 and 3, p. 136-37.
[42] See e.g. KSA 9:15[59].
[43] In this respect, while acknowledging the reality of a more robustly political Nietzsche, my approach obviously inclines towards the sort of apolitical, privatized readings of Walter Kaufmann, *Nietzsche: Philosopher, Psychologist, Antichrist*, 4th ed. (Princeton: Princeton University Press, 1974), pp. 242–56 (cf. p. 418) and Richard Rorty, *Contingency, Irony, and Solidarity* (New York: Cambridge University Press, 1989), esp. chap. 4.
[44] George Eliot, *Middlemarch* (New York, Harper Collins, 2015), p. 838.

Why Nietzsche is a Destiny:
Epicurean Themes in Ecce Homo

Daniel Conway

> This, in fact, is how that long period of sickness appears to me *now*: as it were, I discovered life anew, including myself; I tasted all good and even little things, as others cannot easily taste them—I turned my will to health, to *life*, into a philosophy.
> —Friedrich Nietzsche, *Ecce Homo*, "Wise" 2

Section One

That Nietzsche meant to renew his allegiance to the pursuit of philosophy as a way of life is evident throughout *Ecce Homo* (1888). As his subtitle confirms, he is concerned in this book to demonstrate to his best readers "how one becomes what one is." He does so, as we know, by urging them to "behold the man" he (supposedly) has become, precisely so that they might share in the therapeutic benefits that accrue to the way of life he now exemplifies.[1] Although he sees fit on occasion to generalize from his own experiences, the warrant for the practical advice he dispenses rests solely on the value of the way of life he has perfected. That he has "turned out well" should be sufficient for the readers he seeks (EH "Wise" §2).[2]

That Nietzsche also meant to renew his allegiance to Epicurus is similarly evident in *Ecce Homo*. As he introduces his readers to his new way of life, he rehearses a number of familiar Epicurean themes: a formula for happiness modeled on Epicurean *ataraxia*; a strict determination of what one can and cannot control, including the eventual expiration of one's mortal soul; a therapeutic attunement to the "little things" in life; an elaboration of the remedies that enabled him (and may enable others) to convalesce; an appreciation of the necessity of fate and of the benefits of *loving* fate; a dispensation of practical advice, often in the form of easily repeated maxims; and a renewed effort to discredit the odious teaching of personal (i.e., soul-based) immortality. Much like

---

[1] My attention to the theme of exemplification (via embodiment) in *Ecce Homo* is indebted to the interpretation developed by Nehamas, *Life as Literature*, 192-99; and 230-34.

[2] Nietzsche, F. *On the Genealogy of Morals*, trans. Walter Kaufmann and R.J. Hollingdale, and *Ecce Homo*, trans. Walter Kaufmann. New York: Random House/Vintage Books, 1989.

Epicurus, in fact, Nietzsche recommends his way of life by offering its this-worldly fruits—*behold the man!*—as the only proof that would be needed by the readers he hopes to attract.[3]

At the same time, however, Nietzsche's plan to renew his allegiance to Epicurus is more complicated than it may appear. On the one hand, we know, his pre-Zarathustran writings are generally appreciative of Epicurus and his teachings.[4] In *Human, All Too Human*, for example, Nietzsche praises Epicurus as "wisdom in bodily form" (HH II §224) and as "one of the greatest of men, the inventor of an heroic-idyllic mode of philosophizing" (HH II/2 §295).[5] On the other hand, his post-Zarathustran writings suggest a dramatic revision of his previous estimation of Epicurus. After supposing that Epicurus may have been "afflicted" (BT "Attempt" §1, 4), and that his teachings appealed primarily to kindred "sufferers" (GM II §17), Nietzsche eventually diagnoses Epicurus as a "*typical décadent*," whose "fear of pain, even of infinitely minute pain…can end in no other way than in a *religion of love*" (A §30).[6] Despite its "generous admixture of Greek vitality and nervous energy," in fact, Epicureanism is "most closely related" to the glad tidings of Jesus (A §30).[7]

Rather than choose between these seemingly incompatible interpretations of Epicurus, Nietzsche combines them to produce the idealized self-presentation on display in *Ecce Homo*. On the one hand, he presents himself, like the Epicurus who appears in his pre-Zarathustran writings, as wisdom incarnate, i.e., as an exemplar of the philosophical way of life that he now recommends to his best readers. On the other hand, he also presents himself, like the Epicurus depicted in his post-Zarathustran writings, as a *décadent,* i.e., as burdened by an involuntary inheritance that he is powerless to master or disown. In Nietzsche's own person, that is, we are urged to behold a contradiction or tension that may put us in mind of the Epicurus he has variously described.

Nietzsche's aim in motivating this comparison is to highlight what he takes to be the crucial difference between them. Unlike Epicurus, who apparently had no choice but to accommodate his besetting decay, Nietzsche "opposes" his share in the *décaden*ce that grips the late modern epoch:

[3] See Hadot, *Philosophy as a Way of Life*, 271-75; and Ansell-Pearson, "True to the Earth," 101-09.

[4] See Ansell-Pearson, "True to the Earth," 99-101; and Ansell-Pearson, "Heroic-Idyllic Philosophizing," 253-59.

[5] Nietzsche, F. *Human, All Too Human*, trans. R.J. Hollingdale. Cambridge: Cambridge University Press, 1986.

[6] Nietzsche, F. *The Antichrist*, in *The Portable Nietzsche*, ed. and trans. Walter Kaufmann. New York: Viking Penguin, 1982.

[7] See Conway, "Epicurus Avenged?," 4-7.

> Apart from the fact that I am a *décadent*, I am also the opposite [*Gegensatz*]. My proof for this is, among other things, that I have always instinctively chosen the *right* means against wretched states; while the *décadent* typically chooses means that are disadvantageous for him. (EH "Wise" §2)

This is an important distinction for Nietzsche to mobilize, for he generally and consistently defines *décadence* as a condition in which one instinctively chooses what is least advantageous for one's health and wellbeing. In light of this definition, in fact, his (avowed) ability to choose well for himself proves that he, as opposed to Epicurus, is basically *healthy* (EH "Wise" §2). As a result, he explains, his best readers need not fend for themselves. Translating his solitude and suffering into a positive program of therapeutic remedy, he invites his best readers to adopt *Ecce Homo* as their *vade mecum*.[8]

In typical fashion, Nietzsche renews his allegiance to Epicurus by claiming to surpass him. Epicurus, he now realizes, was every bit as wise and heroic as the pre-Zarathustran writings asserted, even if his appreciation of *ataraxia* was tinctured by the *décadence* that came to light in the post-Zarathustran writings. Despite promising his followers a life of positive pleasures, Epicurus instead delivered a welcome remission of their pain and suffering. What this means, according to Nietzsche, is that Epicurus was *not* a genuine healer or physician. (In his post-Zarathustran writings, Nietzsche levels a similar charge against Socrates, Wagner, the ascetic priest, and virtually every other nemesis he cares to diagnose.)[9]

Unlike Epicurus, who was obliged to accept his decay and rebrand it as "happiness," Nietzsche has remade himself anew, in brazen defiance of the *décadent* trends and norms of his day. Despite being very much a "child of his time" (CW P),[10] he refuses to allow this accident of historical contingency to determine his destiny. As a preliminary outcome of his efforts thus far, he claims in *Ecce Homo* to have performed with respect to himself the "revaluation of all values," which, as he says, he had intended to demand of humankind as a whole (EH "Preface" §1). With any luck, humankind will discover that it, too, is *décadent only* "as an angle, as a speciality," and that it, too, is fundamentally *healthy* (EH "Wise" §2). In that event, presumably, Nietzsche will be remembered not as a "holy man" or "saint," but as the "destiny" [*Schicksal*] he claims to be.

---

[8] I am indebted here to Jensen, *Nietzsche's Philosophy of History*, 184-96.

[9] See Acampora, *Contesting Nietzsche*, 43-49, 192-97.

[10] Nietzsche, F. *The Birth of Tragedy* and *The Case of Wagner*, trans. Walter Kaufmann. New York: Random House/Vintage Books, 1967.

Section Two

Let us turn now to consider some of the prominent Epicurean themes to be found in *Ecce Homo*. For the sake of brevity, I will limit my consideration to four such themes, which correspond to the first four of the *Sovran Maxims* (or *Principal Doctrines*) [*Kuriai Doxai*] of the Epicurean philosophy, as recorded by Diogenes Laërtius.[11]

> SM1.
>
> A blessed and eternal being has no trouble himself and brings no trouble upon any other being; hence he is exempt from movements of anger and partiality, for every such movement implies weakness.[12]

As this famous maxim is meant to confirm, fear of the gods should never be permitted to spoil or disturb one's enjoyment of earthly pleasures. If the gods exist *qua* gods, Epicurus taught, they have no business with us that should cause us consternation.[13] In the spirit of this maxim, Epicurus and Lucretius regularly inveighed against those priests and magi who mongered fear of the gods in order to consolidate their secular authority. According to Nietzsche, in fact, Epicurus and Lucretius were especially effective in discrediting those proto-Christian "*subterranean* cults" in which "concepts of guilt, punishment, and immortality" were promoted (A §58).

In *Ecce Homo*, Nietzsche is concerned both to declare his adherence to the this-worldly religion of Dionysus *and* to discredit pre-emptively any attempt by religious leaders to appropriate him for their otherworldly designs:

> I know my lot. Some day my name will be linked to the memory of something monstrous, of a crisis as yet unprecedented on earth, the most profound collision of conscience, a decision conjured up against everything hitherto believed, demanded, hallowed. I am not a man, I am dynamite.—And for all that, there is nothing in me of a founder of religions—religions are for the rabble; I need to wash my hands after contact with religious people...I don't *want* any "disciples"...I have a terrible fear of being declared *holy* one day...I don't want to be a saint, and would rather be a buffoon...Perhaps I am a buffoon...(EH "Destiny" §1)

---

11   Diogenes Laërtius, *Lives of Eminent Philosophers*, 663-65. See also Konstan.

12   Diogenes Laërtius, *Lives of Eminent Philosophers*, 663.

13   "Letter to Menoeceus," Diogenes Laërtius, *Lives of Eminent Philosophers*, 649-51. See also Nussbaum, *The Therapy of Desire*, 251-57.

Here Nietzsche voices the understandable concern that his (as-yet-unannounced) "revaluation of all values" may be mistakenly associated with the founding of a *religion* (sneer quotes implied). In that event, of course, he too might be pronounced "holy," despite his efforts to promote a way of life that is not reducible to a set of abstract doctrines or teachings.

Like Epicurus and Lucretius, Nietzsche understands *religion* broadly and pejoratively, and in contrast to the worldly way of life he recommends (GM III §17). As this extract confirms, in fact, Nietzsche sees "religion" as a set of beliefs and practices that is designed to exploit the suffering of the "rabble," i.e., those for whom no realistic expectations of salvation or redemption are likely to be formed. Those who are pronounced "holy" are those who have flattered the rabble with reckless promises of personal immortality and otherworldly revenge. To be sure, however, Nietzsche wishes in particular to avoid the clutches of a "religion" that was unknown to Epicurus and Lucretius in its most virulent form: Pauline Christianity. If the humble, unassuming, omni-affirmative Nazarene could be conscripted as "The Crucified One," i.e., as the founder of a religion, and as desirous of unthinking, hate-fueled disciples, how can Nietzsche hope to safeguard *his* prescribed way of life from a similar act of strategic appropriation by a similarly diabolical world-historical genius? The larger worry here is that *any* alternative teaching that is encoded in an exemplified way of life may be ripe for eventual misunderstanding and misappropriation.[14]

Alert to the obvious similarities between himself and Jesus (and Epicurus), Nietzsche proceeds to reveal the difference that most obviously sets him apart from them. Whereas Jesus and Epicurus were physiologically ill disposed toward any act of resistance, struggle, or negation (A §30), Nietzsche introduces himself in *Ecce Homo* as uniquely authorized to carry out "two negations" [*Verneinungen*], which he directs, respectively, against Christian morality and the "good man" whom Christian morality pronounces "supreme" (EH "Destiny" §4).[15] Content earlier in his career to aspire to a posture of indiscriminate, unconditional affirmation (GS §276),[16] Nietzsche presents himself in *Ecce Homo* as secure in his understanding that "negating and destroying are conditions of saying Yes" (EH "Destiny" §4). In other words, he now understands that affirmation is not the opposite of negation, but its prelude.

SM2.

---

[14] Here I follow Nehamas, *Life as Literature*, 231-34.
[15] See Bertram, 286-88; and Hadot, *Philosophy as a Way of Life*, 165-70.
[16] Nietzsche, F. *The Gay Science*, trans. Walter Kaufmann. New York: Random House/Vintage Books, 1974.

> Death is nothing to us; for the body, when it has been resolved into its elements, has no feeling, and that which has no feeling is nothing to us.[17]

In his pre-Zarathustran writings, Nietzsche praises Epicurus for his efforts to dispel the irrational fear of death. Immodestly associating his own teachings with those of Epicurus, he gleefully remarks that "the 'after-death' no longer concerns us!—an unspeakable benefit, which would be felt as such far and wide if it were not so recent.—And Epicurus triumphs anew!" (D §72).[18] In the spirit of Epicurus, moreover, Nietzsche and Zarathustra both extol the practice of "free death," wherein one regards one's inevitable demise not as a transition to a next or better world, nor as a portal guarded by a priestly elite, but as the natural, anticipated conclusion of a life well lived (TI "Skirmishes" §36; Z I §21).[19] Embracing *this* interpretation of death, they believe, will free mortals to sample widely and voraciously from the full menu of worldly pleasures.[20]

While rehearsing these Epicurean themes, however, Nietzsche is also keen to acknowledge the countervailing influence of the Christian acculturation that has shaped the development of European culture over the course of two millennia. In this respect, it may be more accurate to describe his position in *Ecce Homo* as *neo*-Epicurean, for he is determined to account for the intervening, world-historical influence of Paul, the apostle to the Gentiles.[21] Indeed, Nietzsche's most notable departure from the Epicurean orthodoxy is his promulgation of a teaching of (Dionysian) immortality, which he attaches *not* to the individual souls that supposedly are saved (or not) by grace and good works, but to life itself, which, as Zarathustra relates, is *"that which must always overcome itself"* (Z II §12).

As I have argued elsewhere,[22] Nietzsche apparently believes that our protracted training in Christianity has produced in us an indelible taste, habit, and predilection for immortality. Very recently, he insists, our training in Christianity has compelled us to accommodate a distinctly modern (and distinctly scientific) estimation of the value of truth (GS §357).[23] According to Nietzsche, the improbable merger of Christian morality and scientific rigor has positioned us to

---

[17] Diogenes Laërtius, *Lives of Eminent Philosophers*, 665. See Nussbaum, *The Therapy of Desire*, 192-201.

[18] Nietzsche, F. *Daybreak*, trans. R.J. Hollingdale. Cambridge: Cambridge University Press, 1982.

[19] Nietzsche, F. *Twilight of the Idols*, in *The Portable Nietzsche*, ed. and trans. Walter Kaufmann. New York: Viking Penguin, 1982. Nietzsche, F. *Thus Spoke Zarathustra*, in *The Portable Nietzsche*, ed. and trans. Walter Kaufmann. New York: Viking Penguin, 1982.

[20] Here I follow Loeb, *The Death of Nietzsche's Zarathustra*, 76-81.

[21] See Conway, "Epicurus Avenged?," 12-17.

[22] See Conway, "Epicurus Avenged?," 17-23.

[23] See Havas, *Nietzsche's Genealogy*, 166-73; and Ridley, *Nietzsche's Conscience*, 135-42.

renounce the hoariest prejudices of folk psychology, including the scientifically untenable belief in the immortal "soul *atomon*" (BGE §12).[24]

Aiming to exploit this training, Nietzsche offers the readers of *Ecce Homo* an alternative, Dionysian doctrine of immortality.[25] He does so, of course, neither as an abstract teaching nor as a purely academic exercise, but as the embodied truth of his newborn existence. As it turns out, in fact, the story of his life is also the story of his inadvertent, halting progress toward an affirmation of his own immortality—not as a deathless, indestructible soul, but as a contingent (and recurring) configuration of the finite quanta of force arrayed throughout the ceaselessly verging cosmos.[26] Hence his provocative assertion in *Ecce Homo*: "One pays dearly for immortality: one has to die several times while still alive" (EH "Books" z 5).

SM3.

> The magnitude of pleasure reaches its limit in the removal of all pain. When pleasure is present, so long as is uninterrupted, there is no pain either of body or of mind or of both together.[27]

This maxim has been widely debated and, some would say, widely misunderstood. The dominant concern here is that Epicurus appears to equate pleasure in its greatest "magnitude" with the "absence of pain." This concern has led many critics, including Nietzsche (GM III §17), to suppose or conclude that this maxim trades on an unfortunate (and probably unintended) equivocation on the word "pleasure." For Nietzsche, of course, this equivocation is decisive, for it faithfully reflects the *décadence* of Epicurus. In the event that Epicurus has no irreducibly positive account of the experience of pleasure, in excess of "the absence of suffering" (GM III §17), he hardly would qualify as a proper hedonist, much less as a proper epicure.

In defense of this Epicurean maxim and the teaching from which it is distilled, several scholars have recommended the distinction between two sets of circumstances in which pleasure may be experienced: the *kinetic* (or active) and the *katastematic* (or static).[28] The point of this distinction is to claim, on behalf of

---

[24]   Nietzsche, F. *Beyond Good and Evil: Prelude to a Philosophy of the Future*, trans. Walter Kaufmann. New York: Random House/Vintage Books, 1989.

[25]   Here I follow Loeb, *The Death of Nietzsche's Zarathustra*, 38-41.

[26]   See Loeb, *The Death of Nietzsche's Zarathustra*, 186-90.

[27]   Diogenes Laërtius, *Lives of Eminent Philosophers*, 665.

[28]   Here I follow Cooper, *Pursuits of Wisdom*, 229-32. See also Annas, *The Morality of Happiness*, 236-48; and Meyer, *Ancient Ethics*, 98-99.

Epicurus, that the experience of katastematic pleasure attends the aforementioned "absence of pain." As Susan Suavé Meyer explains this point, "Although our sources sometimes abbreviate the definition of *katastematic* pleasure to 'the absence of pain,' the full and proper account is that it is the feeling or awareness of that absence of pain."[29]

For an illustration of what Epicurus wishes to describe as the conditions under which one is likely to experience katastematic pleasure, one need look no further than Nietzsche's description of himself in *Ecce Homo*:

> At this very moment I still look upon my future—an *ample* future!—as upon calm seas: there is no ripple of desire. I do not want in the least that anything should become different than it is; I myself do not want to become different. But that is how I have always lived. I had no wishes. A man over [the age of] forty-four who can say that he never strove for *honors*, for *women*, for *money*!— Not that I lacked them… (EH "Clever" §9)[30]

Here Nietzsche lays claim to an achievement that calls to mind the serene tranquility, or *ataraxia*, which Epicurus proposed as the highest good attainable by mortals. Untroubled by irrational fears and excitations, Nietzsche is free to contemplate his "ample" future.

It is against this Epicurean backdrop, I offer, that we should situate one of Nietzsche's most familiar statements of affirmation. Revealing the extent of his debt to Epicurus (via Diogenes Laërtius) on the topic of *fate*, Nietzsche declares,

> My formula for greatness in a human being is *amor fati*: Not wanting anything to be different, not forwards, not backwards, for all eternity. Not just enduring what is necessary, still less concealing it—all idealism is hypocrisy in the face of what is necessary—but *loving* it…(EH "Clever" §10)

The distinction he draws in this passage, between *enduring* necessity and *loving* it, attests to his appreciation of the experience of katastematic pleasure. Having glimpsed the *necessity* of fate, he has freed himself from the disruptive perturbations that a preoccupation with fate can produce. Having learned in turn to *love* (and not merely endure) the necessity of fate, Nietzsche bears witness to a positive experience of (katastematic) pleasure, attendant to (and in excess of) the absence of suffering.

---

[29] Meyer, *Ancient Ethics*, 98-99. See also Cooper, *Pursuits of Wisdom*, 229-41; and Annas, *The Morality of Happiness*, 188-92.

[30] Here I prefer the Large translation of *Ecce Homo*. Kaufmann's translation omits the final phrase.

Nietzsche proceeds to account for his spiritual rebirth as relatively effortless on his part, and as following a natural logic of maturation (or "fruition") that previously had been unknown to him (EH "Clever" §9). Only now, in fact, and owing to the clarity of retrospection, is he in a credible position to appreciate and recount the story of his life. The moral of this story, moreover, is that one must allow the moral of one's story to emerge on its own schedule. One's path and destiny will reveal themselves in due time, perhaps even in spite of oneself, provided one receives (or grants oneself) the proper conditions of nurture and development. (EH "Clever" §9). As he explains, one is far more likely to do so if one has come to appreciate the "little things" in life as the non-trivial building blocks of an authentic existence (EH "Clever" §10).

Because Nietzsche has waited to tell the story of his life, thereby refusing the premature, inauthentic stories crafted for him by others, he now has a story worthy of sharing with the envisioned readers of *Ecce Homo*. Here Nietzsche places himself in a testimonial lineage of moral philosophy that may be traced back (at least) as far as Socrates himself. The centerpiece of this tradition is the dissemination of an authentic personal narrative, which allows one to present the idiosyncratic course of one's life as potentially relevant for, and inspirational to, others. The goal of this narrative is to establish the intimate connection between one's general moral lessons or teachings and the unimpeachable quality of the life one leads. We might say that the authenticity of the narrative is question is established by the wisdom one displays, as evidenced by one's success in "*having turned out well*" (EH "Wise" §2).

Not surprisingly, the particular therapeutic remedy Nietzsche has devised for himself is rooted in his experience of his own decay, which, as we have seen, he "opposes." Pursuing this remedy has not cured him of his decay (and never would have done so), but it has perfected in him the dual perspective to which he proudly lays claim in *Ecce Homo* (EH "Wise" §1). Able to access the world from the perspectives of "health" and "sickness," respectively, he beholds a level and degree of complexity that is unknown to those (e.g., Epicurus) who command only one or the other of these perspectives. His most notable achievement in this regard is the immanent critique he develops of those *faux* physicians who, like Epicurus, mistakenly see themselves as genuine healers. Owing to his ability "to *reverse perspectives*" (EH "Wise" §1), moreover, Nietzsche is uniquely able to grant these *faux* physicians their due, while refusing to normalize the founding error of their ministry.

We are now in a position to appreciate how Nietzsche arrived at his uniquely ambivalent estimation of Epicurus.[31] As Nietzsche now understands, Epicurus was correct to pursue philosophy as a way of life *and* to extol *ataraxia* as the

---

[31] See Ansell-Pearson, "Heroic-Idyllic Philosophizing," 258-60.

highest human good. Where he went astray, involuntarily and through no apparent fault of his own, was in his presentation of himself as an *exemplar* of this way of life. Like many or most teachers of virtue, that is, Epicurus mistakenly identified himself as a healer in his own right. Unbeknownst to him and his followers, moreover, he cultivated a clientele that was in fact self-selected by the incipient decay of its unsuspecting members. Desperate for a cure, they were content to overlook the difference, if they noticed it at all, between what was promised to them and what they actually received. For his part, Epicurus provided a garden of "modest" delights (GS §45), which served over time to quell their excitations and adjust their expectations.

Truth be told, the *décadent* clients of Epicurus were physiologically unsuited to the experience of katastematic pleasure, which is why he and they typically settled for *ataraxia* in name only. Somewhat surprisingly, however, Nietzsche derives no lasting criticism from his diagnosis of Epicurus as a "typical *décadent*." Even though Epicurus was unable to provide his followers with a positive experience of pleasure, the privative experience he provided was ideally suited to their condition of physiological distress. Sometimes, as Mick Jagger has observed, you get what you need.

SM4.

> Continuous pain does not last long in the flesh; on the contrary, pain, if extreme, is present a very short time, and even that degree of pain which barely outweighs pleasure in the flesh does not last for many days together. Illnesses of long duration even permit of an excess of pleasure over pain in the flesh.[32]

This is the least persuasive of the *Sovran Maxims* we will consider.[33] Nevertheless, support for this maxim may be found in Nietzsche's project of self-presentation in *Ecce Homo*.

Having conducted a lifelong study of pain and suffering, including the mnemotechnics that produce a lasting impression on souls otherwise lacking in memorial capacity (GM II §3), Nietzsche may seem to be an unlikely champion of this particular remedy. According to him, after all, we owe our acquired status as promise-making animals to the ritualized practice, perfected over the span of millennia, of inflicting excruciating doses of memory-enhancing pain. If it were the case that pain does not "last long in the flesh," as this maxim asserts, we would not be persuaded by Nietzsche's genealogical account of the acquisition of memory.

---

[32] Diogenes Laërtius, *Lives of Eminent Philosophers*, 665.
[33] See Cooper, *Pursuits of Wisdom*, 245.

Still, three points bear noting. First, Nietzsche may be inclined to accept a strict, literal interpretation of the maxim in question. While pain is formative only if it is also enduring, he may be willing to concede that "pain does not last long *in the flesh*" when compared to the duration of pain in the soul or mind. As Nietzsche readily acknowledges, after all, a program of mnemotechnics is successful only insofar as the administration of physical suffering eventually produces (or translates into) psychological suffering. Physical cruelty that fails to touch the souls of its intended recipients may be enjoyable to inflict, as he allows, but it does not further nature's plan to breed a memorial animal (GM II §1).

Second, Nietzsche correctly understood that human beings do not flee or eschew suffering *per se*, but only those instances of suffering that defy reasonable explanation and/or justification. If we believe that instances of pain and suffering make good sense, owing to their supposed necessity or instrumental value, we will gladly embrace them. As Nietzsche reveals, the genius of the ascetic priest lies precisely in his poetic capacity to spin a credible narrative,[34] on the strength of which his sufferers come to see themselves as *sinners*, i.e., as fully deserving of the suffering they endure. In truth, the ascetic priest has only the one trick in his black bag: He urges his clients to scan their souls, searching for particular defects and flaws, and he helps them to find within themselves the source or cause of their discontents. Once placed within a trusty narrative context of justification, that is, even life-long torments will become tolerable, if not downright pleasurable.

Third, Nietzsche actually provides us with a technique for limiting the duration of unwanted bouts of physical suffering. As we know, *Ecce Homo* delivers a tale of protracted struggle, torment, suffering, and pain. In the telling of the tale, however, Nietzsche displays his command of a perspective from which the totality of his suffering may be understood to be ingredient to his various achievements and self-overcomings. The perspective in question is unmistakably autumnal, focused as it is on the seasonal labors associated with the harvest, and Nietzsche's birthday provides a "perfect" occasion to pause and survey the fruits of the expired year. As he calmly and coolly recounts the yield of his harvest, we detect no trace of bitterness, disappointment, resentment, or regret. (As if to punctuate this point, he later declares himself "free of *ressentiment*" (EH "Wise" §6).) In short, his "pain in the flesh" has abated, just as Epicurus predicted it would. He now understands and even affirms the contributions of his suffering to the emergence of the "man" he urges his readers to "behold."

Hence Nietzsche's well known adaptation of the Epicurean maxim in question: *What does not destroy me makes me stronger* (TI "Maxim" §8). Even excruciating pain may be endured *if* it is regarded in retrospect, and *if* it is situated

---

[34]   I am indebted here to Ridley, *Nietzsche's Conscience*, 54-57.

in the context of a larger process of growth, maturation, and fortification. Of course, it will not suffice simply to relate any old story that comes to mind, or to concoct an expedient narrative for a particular purpose (*à la* Scheherazade). Nietzsche's point here, as he occasionally insists, is that *embodiment* is the final proof of truth. One's personal story must fit the incarnate life it narrates, and it must compel our attention by dint of the authenticity it communicates. As Alexander Nehamas has so persuasively suggested, one becomes what one is when one becomes the kind of person who may look back upon the totality of one's life and say, with Nietzsche, "*ecce homo.*"[35]

The final moment of triumph arrives when one may sincerely express one's gratitude for all that life has delivered, pains and pleasures alike. The expression of unmitigated gratitude, or so I offer on Nietzsche's behalf, is a signal index of the experience of katastematic pleasure that accompanies the cessation of pain. Against this Epicurean backdrop, let us revisit the interleaf epigraph to *Ecce Homo*:

> On this perfect day, when everything is ripening and not only the grape turns brown, the eye of the sun just fell upon my life: I looked back, I looked forward, and never saw so many and such good things at once. It was not for nothing that I buried my forty-fourth year today; I had the right to bury it; whatever was life in it had been saved, is immortal…*How could I fail to be grateful to my whole life?*—and so I tell my life to myself. (EH "Epigraph")[36]

Works Cited

Acampora, C. *Contesting Nietzsche*. Chicago: University of Chicago Press, 2013.

Annas, J. *The Morality of Happiness*. New York: Oxford University Press, 1993.

Ansell-Pearson, K. "Heroic-Idyllic Philosophizing: Nietzsche and the Epicurean Tradition." *Royal Institute of Philosophy Supplement*, 74, 2014, 237-263.

— "True to the Earth: Nietzsche's Epicurean Care of Self and World," in *Nietzsche's Therapeutic Teaching: For Individuals and Culture*, eds. Horst Hutter and Eli Friedland. Bloomsbury Academic (Reprint Edition), 2015, 97-116.

Bertram, E. *Nietzsche: Attempt at a Mythology*. Trans. Robert E Norton. Urbana and Champaign, IL: University of Illinois Press, 2009.

Conway, D. "Epicurus Avenged?" *Pli: The Warwick Journal of Philosophy* 1/2 (2016), 3-24.

---

[35] Nehamas, *Life as Literature*, 194-99; 232-34. If we apply a minor tweak to the influential interpretation developed by Nehamas, substituting "life as narrative" for "life as literature," the Epicurean provenance and therapeutic aim of Nietzsche's project in *Ecce Homo* will emerge more fully.

[36] I am grateful to Keith Ansell-Pearson for his comments on an earlier version of this essay.

Cooper, J. *Pursuits of Wisdom: Six Ways of Life in Ancient Philosophy from Socrates to Plotinus*. Princeton: Princeton University Press, 2012.

Diogenes Laërtius. *Lives of Eminent Philosophers*, Vol. II. Trans. R.D. Hicks. Cambridge, MA: Harvard University Press, 1931.

Hadot, P. *Philosophy As a Way of Life*. Ed. and Intro, A. Davidson, trans. M. Chase. Malden, MA: Blackwell, 1995.

Havas, R. *Nietzsche's Genealogy: Nihilism and the Will to Knowledge*. Ithaca, NY: Cornell University Press, 1995.

Jensen, A. *Nietzsche's Philosophy of History*. Cambridge: Cambridge University Press, 2013.

Konstan, D. "Epicurus", *The Stanford Encyclopedia of Philosophy* (Fall 2016 Edition), Edward N. Zalta (ed.), URL = <https://plato.stanford.edu/archives/fall2016/entries/epicurus/>

Loeb, P. *The Death of Nietzsche's Zarathustra*. Cambridge: Cambridge University Press, 2010.

Meyer, S. *Ancient Ethics: A Critical Introduction*. London: Routledge, 2008.

Nehamas, A. *Nietzsche: Life as Literature*. Cambridge, MA: Harvard University Press, 1985.

Nietzsche, F. *Sämtliche Werke: Kritische Studienausgabe in 15 Bänden*, ed. G. Colli and M. Montinari. Berlin: dtv/de Gruyter, 1980.

—*The Gay Science*, trans. Walter Kaufmann. New York: Random House/Vintage Books, 1974.

—*Thus Spoke Zarathustra*, in *The Portable Nietzsche*, ed. and trans. Walter Kaufmann. New York: Viking Penguin, 1982.

—*Twilight of the Idols*, in *The Portable Nietzsche*, ed. and trans. Walter Kaufmann. New York: Viking Penguin, 1982.

—*The Antichrist*, in *The Portable Nietzsche*, ed. and trans. Walter Kaufmann. New York: Viking Penguin, 1982.

—*Daybreak*, trans. R.J. Hollingdale. Cambridge: Cambridge University Press, 1982.

—*Human, All Too Human*, trans. R.J. Hollingdale. Cambridge: Cambridge University Press, 1986.

—*Beyond Good and Evil: Prelude to a Philosophy of the Future*, trans. Walter Kaufmann. New York: Random House/Vintage Books, 1989.

—*On the Genealogy of Morals*, trans. Walter Kaufmann and R.J. Hollingdale, and *Ecce Homo*, trans. Walter Kaufmann. New York: Random House/Vintage Books, 1989.

—*Ecce Homo*, trans. Duncan Large. Oxford: Oxford University Press, 2007.

Nussbaum, M. *The Therapy of Desire*. Princeton, NJ: Princeton University Press, 1994.

Ridley, A. *Nietzsche's Conscience: Six Character Studies From the* Genealogy. Ithaca, NY: Cornell University Press, 199

Pleasure and Self-Cultivation in Guyau and Nietzsche

Federico Testa & Matthew Dennis

Guyau and Nietzsche: Brothers in Arms?

Until recently Jean-Marie Guyau only made a slight mark in the history of philosophy in the Anglophone world, although his work has been significantly more prominent in the Francophone tradition. Such an oversight is inexplicable if one thinks back to the avid reception of Guyau's work in the late 1870s and early 1880s.[1] By the time of his premature death at 33 years old, Guyau was a well-known figure in France, to some extent due to the steadfast championing of his life-long mentor and interlocutor, Alfred Fouillée. While Fouillée's promotion helped create an explosion of receptive literature in France during Guyau's lifetime, many contemporary philosophical heavyweights also engaged with his work, including Henri Bergson,[2] Emile Durkheim,[3] Herbert Spencer,[4] and the anarchist thinker Piotr Kropotkin.[5] Furthermore, even after Guyau's death in 1888, interest in Guyau's work remained strong enough that Harald Høffding,

---

[1] While Guyau's French reception was deeply approving, even some influential voices from the English-speaking philosophical world were supportive. See Henry Sidgwick's glowing review of the newly-published *La morale d'Épicure*, for example, in Sidgwick, H. (1879). *Mind*, IV (16): 582–587. Or, after Guyau's death, Thomas Whittaker's and James Sully's approving comments on his life's work (and Fouillée introduction to him) in Whittaker, T. (1889). *Mind*, XIV (54): 295–296, and Sully, J. (1890). *Mind*, XV (58): 279–284.

[2] According to Schöpke, Bergson collaborated in the posthumous edition of Guyau's *La genèse de l'idée de temps* (Schöpke 2007: 8).

[3] Accoring to Riba, 'Gabriel Aslan presented his thesis *La morale selon Guyau* at the Sorbonne in the 10th of March 1906', Emile Durkheim was one of the examiners composing the panel. Durkheim also discussed Guyau's conceptions of anomy, as well as his thought on religion. Cf. Durkheim, E. 'Guyau. L'irreligion de l'avenir, étude de sociologie', *Revue Philosophique* XXIII, 1887 (Riba 1999: 299–311).

[4] Riba says Spencer read Guyau with enthusiasm. According to Spencer, Guyau was the first to describe his ethics with an acute precision (Riba 1999: 8). Cf. Guyau's 'L'hérédité morale et M. Spencer', *Revue philosophiquee de la France et de l'étranger*, quatrième année, tome VII. (Guyau 1879: 308–315).

[5] See Kropotkine 'L'Éthique, chapitre 13' (Guyau 2012b).

the Danish historian of philosophy, thought it fitting to devote a sizable entry to Guyau in his influential *A Brief History of Modern Philosophy*,[6] sandwiching a synopsis of Guyau's major works between similarly-sized entries on William James and Friedrich Nietzsche.

Despite catching the attention of figures like Høffding, Guyau's influence penetrated significantly deeper into nineteenth-century philosophy than featuring in the philosophical anthologies of this era. Partly on account of the scope of topics that Guyau engaged in, partly because of the contemporary relevance of his project, his work directly influenced some of the twentieth century's greatest thinkers, including philosophical giants such as Bergson and Nietzsche. As early as 1902, Fouillée compared Nietzsche and Guyau, heavily criticizing what he understood as the elitism and conservative aristocratic views of the former,[7] and claiming that although Guyau is one of Nietzsche's processors he 'does not fall into the errors of Nietzsche' (1902: 19).

Recently – in a less polemical line – a new wave of Guyau scholarship has focused on Guyau's influence on Nietzsche, which has been shown to be subtle but significant. A bi-lingual edition (French and German) of Guyau's *A Sketch of Morality Independent of Obligation or Sanction*[8] was published in 2012, which includes Nietzsche's (mostly strongly approving) marginalia from his personal copy of this text.[9] Guyau's *Sketch of Morality*, often read in conjunction with Nietzsche's marginalia, has provided the first point of comparison between these two thinkers

---

[6] Høffding, H. (1894). *Den nyere Filosofis Historie*. Copenhagen: Gyldendal. Translated into English as *A Brief History of Modern Philosophy* by C. F. Sander in 1900. See especially pp. 304–06 dealing with Guyau, and the subsequent section on Nietzsche.

[7] Fouillée says Nietzsche was 'a false spirit', a *'partisan* of force' and an 'enemy of every democracy' (Fouillée 1902: 16). Despite its heavy tone, Fouillée's criticism seems very lucid, especially if we consider the historical appropriations of Nietzsche, in which fascist ideologues celebrated exactly the points which Fouillée attacks, and which in his view separate Guyau from Nietzsche. For Fouillée, Guyau prefigures Nietzschean critique of morality, without carrying its dangerous virtualities. It is also interesting to contrast Fouillée's critique to an English reception by Knight in 1933, who emphasises a different aspect of Nietzsche's thought, in contrast with the German appropriations at the time. See Knight, A.H.J. (1933). 'Nietzsche and Epicurean Philosophy', *Philosophy* 8 (32): 431–45. See Ansell-Pearson (2014a: 4).

[8] *Esquisse d'une morale sans obligation ni sanction.*

[9] Jean-Marie Guyau, (2012a) *Mit den Annotationen von Friedrich Nietzsche: Rekonstruktion der kritischen Lektüre von Friedrich Nietzsche mit Marginalien*, Ilse Walther-Dulk (ed.), Weimar: *Verlag und Datenbank für Geisteswissenschaften*. See also the French edition reproducing Nietzsche's notes: Guyau, J.-M. (2012). *Esquisse d'une morale sans obligation ni sanction: avec les textes de Nietzsche et Kropotkine*. Paris: Payot et Rivages.

for this recent wave of Guyau-Nietzsche scholarship,[10] although we hope to show below that there are also informative comparisons to be made by putting Guyau's *La morale d'Épicure*[11] alongside Nietzsche's middle period writings on Epicurus.

Nietzsche's bibliographical records do not reveal whether he read *The Ethics of Epicurus*, so any comparative approach must rely on overlaps and synchronicities between his and Guyau's texts. Such overlaps are both methodological and thematic. As well as patent similarities in thematic concerns (pleasure, life, self-cultivation), Nietzsche's middle period works are methodologically heterodox insofar as they bring to bear the results of recent natural science (Darwinism, Lamarckism) and new modes of historical enquiry (genealogy)[12] to his most pressing philosophical concerns in ethics and axiology. As we will see, Guyau's method is equally as synergistic, since he seeks to apply his knowledge of classical philosophy to new developments in natural science, both aiming to show how recent scientific discoveries can corroborate the philosophical claims of Epicureanism, as well as showing how scientific developments often further ancient lines of inquiry.

In *The Ethics of Epicurus*, Guyau's interpretative enterprise is twofold: on the one hand, he engages in an effort of systematic interpretation of ancient philosophy; on the other he distances himself of an antiquarian approach, by taking up the task of unfolding questions that ancient thought could present to modern ethics. Although these two vectors clearly mark Guyau's interpretation of Epicurean philosophy, *La morale d'Épicure* could as well be characterized by a movement which surpasses the history of ideas in the direction of reviving the ancient, especially Hellenistic, idea of 'philosophy as a way of life'. Guyau is concerned with the way in which we can live a fulfilled life, the ways in which we could cultivate ourselves in order to resist superstition, fear, and death. For him, rational emancipation is at the core of Epicurus' system.

As we will see, Guyau found in Epicurus what, according to Keith Ansell-Pearson, Nietzsche found in the ancient philosopher after him, namely an 'ethos of Epicurean enlightenment',[13] for '[i]n the middle-period, Epicurus is one of

---

[10] See Ansell-Pearson, K. (2009). 'Free spirits and free thinkers: Nietzsche and Guyau on the Future of Morality.' In Jeffrey A. Metzger (ed.), *Nietzsche, Nihilism, and the Philosophy of the Future*. Continuum, pp. 102–124. More recently, see Ansell-Pearson, K. (2015). 'Beyond Obligation? Jean-Marie Guyau on Life and Ethics'. *Royal Institute of Philosophy Supplement*, 77: 207–225.

[11] *The Ethics of Epicurus*.

[12]

[13] 'My contention is that an ethos of Epicurean enlightenment pervades Nietzsche's middle period texts with Epicurus celebrated for his teachings on morality and the

Nietzsche's chief inspirations in his effort to liberate himself from the metaphysical need, to find serenity within his own existence, and to help humanity in its need now to cure its neuroses' (Ansell-Pearson 2013: 104). In 1933, A.H.J Knight inaugurated this interpretative line in the English context, claiming that 'Epicurus and Nietzsche are both liberators of human life from religious superstition and mystification, and both place ethics at the centre of philosophy' (Knight 1933: 437).[14] We believe the same can be said of Guyau's *The Ethics of Epicurus.*

In terms of methodology, both Guyau and middle-period Nietzsche propose a reflective and critical approach to the history of philosophy, one that aims to support each of their versions of ethical naturalism with the empirical findings of contemporary science. Just as Nietzsche fashions the source material for his middle-period work into an original set of philosophical theories, so too Guyau uses the approaches of utilitarianism and evolutionary theory to explain his markedly unorthodox reading of Epicurus's philosophy, and to offer us an updated account of Epicureanism for the modern world.

In this introductory article we will sketch the key dimensions of Guyau's and Nietzsche's readings of Epicurus in order to contextualize the translation of *The Ethics of Epicurus* which appears in English for the first time below.[15] We contend that reading Nietzsche and Guyau on Epicurus in tandem gives us greater insight into how Epicurus is a vital philosophical influence on Nietzsche's middle period, as well as allowing us to understand Nietzsche's well-known criticisms of Epicurus in his later work. We begin by examining some of the most brutal criticisms of Nietzsche's alleged Epicureanism in the second volume of Heidegger's monograph on Nietzsche, and argue that these criticisms are not only textually tenuous but also cannot account for the pervasive influence of Epicurus on Nietzsche's conception of philosophical self-cultivation which he retains throughout his work. After this we introduce *The Ethics of Epicurus*, identifying Guyau's characterization of the Epicurean sage as an 'artist of existence' as in

---

cultivation of modest pleasures [...] The aim of philosophy for Nietzsche is to temper emotional and mental excess, and here Epicurus' teaching has a key role to play'. Ansell-Pearson (2014a: 7).

[14] Ansell-Pearson 2014a: 5. See also Knight, A. H. J. (1933). 'Nietzsche and Epicurean Philosophy', *Philosophy*, 8: 437.

[15] A first English translation of the conclusion to *The Ethics of Epicurus* was made by Mitchell Abidor. His translation is available at the Marxist Internet Archive: https://www.marxists.org/archive/guyau/1878/epicurus.htm. We would like to thank Mitchell for providing us with useful information about Guyau and relevant sources.

some ways precursory to Nietzsche's understanding of the active and rational processes of philosophical self-cultivation.

Nietzsche's Epicurus

Perhaps it is no accident that commentators who emphasise the importance of Nietzsche's later writings and *Nachlass* view his relationship with Epicurus as predominantly negative. In a 1884–86 note in *The Will to Power* Nietzsche tells us that he regards "Epicurean delight' (*Vergnügen*) [as] out of the question' because he now believes that '[o]nly 'Dionysian joy' (*Lust*) is sufficient' for his understanding of 'the tragic' (KSA 11.25 [95]; WP 1029). As Joseph Vincenzo notes, Heidegger emphasises how Nietzsche regards Epicurus' influence on the history of philosophy as woefully deleterious, which Heidegger argues can be seen if we pay attention to the allegorical nature of the chapter entitled 'The Convalescent' in *Thus Spoke Zarathustra* (Vincenzo 1994: 384). On Heidegger's account, when Zarathustra's animals tell Zarathustra that, '[t]he world outside is like a garden that awaits him' (Heidegger 1984 [1961]: 52), we must understand this claim as a reference to Epicurus' garden as well as to the ethical ideal of *ataraxia* which Epicurus promotes. Zarathustra, Heidegger claims, is rightly sceptical towards this promise as he is able to see beyond the seductions of the *ataraxic* ideal, which merely beautifies the 'terrible thing that being *is*'. Zarathustra, on this reading, knows the 'world is no garden […] especially if by 'garden' we mean an enchanting haven from the flight from being'. To support this interpretation – which is much needed since there is no direct reference to Epicurus in Nietzsche's original passage – Heidegger invokes KSA 7.368, an unpublished note from 1882–84, which includes an apparently dismissive reference to 'gardens'.[16] Heidegger uses this to support his claim that 'Nietzsche's conception of the world does not provide the thinker with a sedate residence in which he can putter about unperturbed, like the philosopher of old, Epicurus, in his 'garden'' (Heidegger 1984 [1961]: 52).

While readings such as Heidegger's were influential for initial scholarship on Nietzsche's relationship to Epicurus, over the last decade they have been challenged by a wave of new commentaries that stress the importance of Hellenistic ideas in Nietzsche's middle period. Rather than emphasising Nietzsche's own biographical remarks from 1885 onwards, in which he tells us

---

[16] Heidegger 1984 [1961]: 52. '*Solitude for a time* necessary, in order that the creature be totally permeated – cured and hard. New forms of community, asserting itself in a warlike manner. Otherwise the spirit grows soft. No 'gardens' and no sheer 'evasion in the face of the masses.' War (but without gunpowder!) between different thoughts! And their armies!' (Nietzsche KSA 7.368)

that he had 'gradually came to understand Epicurus [as] the antithesis of a Dionysian pessimist' and a proto-Christian,[17] this scholarship has sought to show that Nietzsche not only regards the historical Epicurus as an ally, but that (like Guyau) he was also inspired by the quintessentially Epicurean themes of pleasure and ascetic moderation, friendship and sociality, as well as rational practices of self-cultivation. Such claims complement recent and persuasive work on the Stoic influence on Nietzsche's engagement with these themes (Ure 2008, 2009; Nussbaum 2011), and aim to redress the balance of Hellenistic influences that were crucial to Nietzsche at this time. Both Nietzsche and Guyau do not merely take up a Hellenistic philosopher as an object of study, but also aim to show how this transforms philosophical activity, especially insofar as Hellenistic thinkers such as Epicurus offer techniques of self-cultivation that have the potential to be reactualized today.

The evidence that middle-period Nietzsche regarded himself as close to Epicurus, and aligned with Epicureanism, is copious and persuasive. He frequently makes approving references to the ancient philosopher from the beginning of the second edition of *Human All Too Human* (AOM §224; AOM §408; WS §112; WS §227; WS §295),[18] as well as writing warmly of him in his correspondence with Peter Gast (also an Epicurus-enthusiast) at this time. For instance, on January 22nd 1879 he confides to Gast that, 'I live on the whole […] with the outlook of the complete, genuine Epicurus – with my soul very calm and patient and yet contemplating life with joy'.[19] Furthermore, in the 1882 edition of *The Gay Science*, he dedicates a whole aphorism, '*Epicurus*', to the Hellenistic philosopher, telling us that:

> I am proud to experience Epicurus' character in a way unlike perhaps anyone else and to enjoy, in everything I hear and read of him, the happiness of the afternoon of antiquity: I see his eye gaze at a wide whitish sea, across shoreline rocks bathed in the sun, as large and small creatures play in its light, secure and calm like the light and his eye itself.[20]

GS §45 reveals much of what Nietzsche thinks he shares with Epicurus. While the initial gilded imagery might suggest this would be a mutual love of pleasure,

---

[17] 'The 'Christian' […] is really simply a kind of Epicurean' (GS §370).
[18] See also D §453 and GS §45.
[19] See also Nietzsche's letter to Gast on July 1st 1883. Here he reports (figuratively, we can assume) that he has 'once again contemplated Epicurus' bust' and has found 'strength of will and spiritually […] expressed in the head to the highest degree'.
[20] GS §45. Nietzsche, F. (1974) [1882]. *The Gay Science*, trans. W. Kaufmann. Vintage.

in the second half of the aphorism Nietzsche tells us that he believes Epicurus' account of pleasure was unique because (until perhaps his own account) 'never before has voluptuousness been so modest'. Admiring the transformative power of Epicurean simple pleasures – instead heady narcotic pleasures which Nietzsche typically rallies against[21] – is a constant theme in the middle period, although as we will see it is the pleasure's potential role in self-cultivation that interests Nietzsche most.

As Ansell-Pearson suggests, rather than misreading Epicurus as a philosopher of indulgent hedonism, Nietzsche's middle-period writings promote an 'Epicurean-inspired care of self' because he writes as if he regards pleasure as only useful insofar as it has the capacity to further one's own cultivation (2013: 97). This position marks a convergence with Guyau, who says that even if pleasures are always good in themselves for Epicurus, they must be subordinated to a higher goal: happiness, and the cultivation of a beautiful life.[22] Similarly, Nietzsche dismisses pleasures that have no therapeutic or self-cultivationary function as decadent, and his dismissals gain greater force in his unpublished writings of the 1880s.[23] Several years earlier, in a passage that echoes Guyau's critique of Cyrenaic hedonism, Nietzsche tells us that the problem with bestial or 'animal' pleasures is that they are 'so strong that they reduce the intellect to silence or to servitude' (GS §3) in a way that makes them incompatible with the intellectual self-cultivation of 'higher types'. While those who deliberately suffuse their lives with such pleasures can readily identify with others who similarly 'succumb to the passion of the belly [*Leidenschaft des Bauches*]', for example, they 'cannot comprehend' why higher types strive to attain 'objects whose value seems quite fantastic and arbitrary [such as] the passion for knowledge [*Leidenschaft der Erkenntniss*]' (GS §3). Comments such as this support contention that, instead of promoting indulgent bodily pleasures for their own sake, Nietzsche's 'cultivation of modest pleasures' has a primarily therapeutic purpose as it aims to 'temper emotional and mental excess' that according to Epicurus is naturally associated with unrestrained indulgence (Ansell-Pearson 2014a: 3).

Understanding middle-period Nietzsche as interested in Epicurus insofar as he regards the latter's account of modest pleasure as a useful mode of self-cultivation, helps us to re-evaluate his later criticisms, while also showing how the target of these attacks has subtly changed. Although these attacks are directed

---

[21] See GS §3 and GS §12.
[22] See Guyau 1878: 40-41.
[23] In the 1880s, Nietzsche he characterises excessive gustatory pleasure, 'erotic precociousness', and the habit of drinking alcohol as 'decadent' (KSA 13.15[80]; WP §49).

towards Epicurus' ethical ideal of *ataraxia*, none of these criticisms touch on those practices and virtues of self-cultivation that Nietzsche draws inspiration from in his middle-period work. Nevertheless, Nietzsche's final claims that Epicurus is the 'antithesis of a Dionysian pessimist', or that the modern-day Christian is actually 'simply a kind of Epicurean' (GS §370), may not be as severe as they first appear. As we have seen, in his later work, one of Nietzsche's most cutting criticisms of Epicurus is that ethically he is a 'proto-Christian', whose teachings are only superior to latter-day Christianity because they are not supported by the implausible metaphysics of the Christian tradition. This suggests that although Nietzsche eventually renounces Epicurus, his post-1886 work could be said to remain influenced by him insofar as he as does not explicitly renounce a conception of ethical self-cultivation.[24]

As we will see, Guyau's revised-Epicureanism overlaps with Nietzsche insofar as he also picks up on philosophical practices of self-cultivation. For Guyau, not only does Epicureanism inspire a hidden history of philosophy stretching from Gassendi to Hobbes, from Spinoza to the French Moralists, but it also has the potential to underwrite a new revitalised version of Epicureanism for modern philosophy. As we will see, Guyau's understanding of the self-cultivationary use of pleasure has much in common with Nietzsche's work in the middle period.

Guyau's Method in *La Morale d'Épicure*

Epicureanism is, for Guyau, a refined *art of happiness* through which we can liberate ourselves from the servitude to the passions, filling our lives with a superior form of beauty, in the same way that the artist creates a work of art which stands for itself.[25] The emancipatory work of reason and aesthetics of existence

---

[24] One could rightly object that Nietzsche does not emphasise the use of moderate pleasure as he did in his middle-period writings. If on the one hand, we believe it is possible to note a subtle permanence of the theme self-cultivation (e.g. the culinary metaphors in EH); on the other, we must note the fact that Nietzsche's tenor and tone in this period emphasises risk, struggle, and the overall dissolution of the sovereign self (as emphasised by authors as Bataille, Blanchot and Foucault) – recovering the themes of *tragedy* and of a 'Dionysian worldview' of his early writings, now understood within a philosophy of power and will to power. In a footnote to the *Gay Science*, Walter Kaufmann says that 'Nietzsche's reason for finally being dissatisfied with Epicurus is stated most succinctly in *The Will to Power*, note 1029: "I have presented such terrible images to knowledge that any 'Epicurean delight' is out of the question. Only Dionysian joy is sufficient" In the end, Nietzsche was not willing to renounce enthusiasm and passion.' (Nietzsche 1974: 111-112).

[25] Guyau. *La morale d'Épicure*, Book 1, chapter III, (Guyau 1878: 42). The analogy is with painting.

form a single picture in Guyau's view of Epicurus, for, as he says, the Epicurean sage 'contemplates and admires this artwork which is simultaneously beautiful and rational' (1878: 42). Before presenting Guyau's view of the sage as the artist of happiness, who mobilizes pleasure as an instrument of a self-cultivationary process, let us introduce some of the particularities of Guyau's *demarche* in *La morale d'Épicure*.

Guyau's history of philosophy in *La morale d'Épicure* aims to be an untimely and engaged intervention in the philosophical debate of his time. Guyau draws comparisons between important positions in the ancient and modern debates, revealing similarities, hidden kinships, and continuities.[26] Perhaps we could say that Guyau's method also mobilizes a sort of prudent art of *anachronism*,[27] reading ancient philosophy from the perspective of modernity, and vice-versa.[28] Guyau's procedure consists in allowing the contemporary to emerge in the surface of ancient, but also in allowing the ancient to emerge in the contemporary.

For Guyau, the historian must study philosophies as living systems.[29] The historian must reconstruct these systems, starting from their fundamental structures, or 'key ideas'.[30] Once those structures are identified and articulated, the historian has to follow their 'path' of development and growth, that is, the dynamic life and movement of those 'key ideas' in time. A special feature of Guyau's account of the history of Western ethical thought is the quasi meta-

---

[26] For example, Guyau sees the *éthique de l'intérêt* as both contemporary and ancient: 'The ethics of interest [*éthique de l'intérêt*], espoused for a hundred years by the greatest French thinkers and the English philosophers, is not such a historical novelty. We know that a similar doctrine – under the name of Epicureanism – seduced antiquity'. For Guyau, the Epicurean calculus of pleasures and pains, aiming at achieving happiness, prefigures the emergence of utilitarianism.

[27] I take the idea of *anachronism* from Georges Didi-Huberman. In *Devant le temps* (2000), he develops the concept in a particular approach to the history of art.

[28] Guyau's approach consists in [i] projecting forwards ancient standards, showing how ancient philosophies lie historically before modern positions (e.g. showing that modern utilitarianism is a continuation of ancient Epicureanism), but also [ii] projecting backwards contemporary standards (e.g. showing that Epicureanism is a form of utilitarianism, or that it could be read from the perspective of evolutionism and positivism). I thank Matthew Sharpe for pointing out some problems in the use of the term 'anachronism' in Guyau's case.

[29] 'Once one views a system from within, one can see its birth, its gradual growth, and evolution, similar to how one can observe such a life cycle in a living being' (Guyau 1878: 5). For an analysis of the implications and philosophical grounds of this analogy and of Guyau's method, especially regarding the arts. See Testa, 2011.

[30] 'First, one should grasp the key idea [*idée maîtresse*] of the doctrine' (Guyau 1878: 4).

historical place occupied by Epicureanism. In this regard, we could say of Guyau what Lampert says of Nietzsche when he claims that his recovery of Epicurus 'forms a key component in his new history of philosophy'.[31] To explain this pivotal role of Epicureanism in the history of thought, in the introduction to *The Ethics of Epicurus* Guyau tells us that:

> It is Epicureanism [...] that is born again with Helvétius, d'Holbach, Saint-Lambert. It is Epicureanism that inspires all the French writers of the eighteenth century [...] Then it returns in England, gathering in Hobbes' homeland even more numerous *partisans*. With Bentham and Mill, it assumes its definitive form, which... is not that different from its original source. Finally, with Spencer and Darwin it grows anew. To the more or less transformed moral system of Epicurus, a wide cosmological system is added: new Democritians provide modern Epicureans with the means to ground their ethics in the laws of the whole universe, encompassing man and the universe in a same conception (1878:13).

Guyau shows how Epicureanism reappears, here and there, in scientific discoveries and philosophical innovations. For him, as for Nietzsche, 'Epicurus has been alive in all ages and he lives now' (KSA 10.7 [151]).[32] Nevertheless, if Epicureanism appears to Guyau as this fundamental force propelling the movement of thought, we must add that he does not describe this movement as a peaceful, conciliatory dialectics, but rather as an agonistic conflict between distinct forces. He explains:

> Epicurus' influence, which has remained considerable since the last century, is increasing despite the new Stoicism of Kant and his school. Everywhere, in theory and practice, we find [these] two moral philosophies [*morales*]... split philosophical thought and divide human beings. We could say that today the fierce half-a-millennium struggle between the Epicureans and the Stoics has rekindled and is burning anew (Guyau 1878:13).

---

[31] Lampert, L. (1993). *Nietzsche and Modern Times: A Study of Bacon, Descartes, and Nietzsche*. New Haven: Yale University Press: 'Epicurus becomes a central figure. Rethinking Epicurus led to essential advances in the new physio-psychology. Reciprocally, those advances required the whole history of philosophy to be reordered' (Lampert 1993: 395). Also see: 'The new future [...] reestablishes the proper relationship between science and philosophy by reinterpreting the history of philosophy, and in particular, Epicurus' (Lampert 1993: 389). See Ansell-Pearson 2012: 100.

[32] Ansell-Pearson, 2013: 97.

For Guyau, Stoicism and Epicureanism are not just two ancient philosophical schools, but also two fundamental forces or philosophical passions in permanent opposition, elements of an unsolvable tension, which fuels the development of thought and morality. If, this recurring *agon* between Stoicism and Epicureanism characterizes our ways of thinking and practicing philosophy, Guyau's approach is not neutral but *partisan*, situating himself on the side of Epicureanism.[33]

The fierce opposition between these two moral doctrines only loses intensity through the intervention of a third force, that which Guyau calls 'religious enthusiasm'.[34] In Guyau's reconstruction, religious enthusiasm, as well as the superstition and fear it inspires, is the first target of the Epicurean project of liberation. In a strikingly modern way of considering the emancipatory potential of science, Guyau claims that Epicureanism – analogously to the positivism and

---

[33] As he says, 'Their adversaries, the Stoics, vainly struggled against the Epicureans and this struggle lasted for the duration of the Roman Empire. The Stoics, however, could neither weaken nor defeat the Epicureans, nor could they escape their influence' (1878:12). Nietzsche in WS 227 also speaks of a complementarity of Epicureanism and Stoicism – 'Epicurus relate to the Stoics as beauty does to sublimity; but one would have to be a Stoic at the very least to catch sight of this beauty'. See also Hadot who tell us: 'In the *Metaphysics of Morals* (theory of ethical method), Kant declares that the exercise of virtue must be practiced with Stoic energy and Epicurean *joie de vivre*. This conjunction of Stoicism and Epicureanism can be found in Rousseau's *Reveries of a Solitary Walker*, in which there is both the pleasure of existing and the awareness of being part of nature. Goethe describes beings who, by their innate tendencies, are half Stoic and half Epicurean.' And one can also make out an attitude of this kind in Thoreau's *Walden*. In a posthumous fragment, Nietzsche says that one must not be scared of adopting a Stoic attitude after having benefited from an Epicurean recipe.' Ultimately, an attitude like this one is what is called *eclecticism*. This word is often rather poorly viewed by philosophers. In general, from Kant to Nietzsche, we have spoken of Stoicism and Epicureanism. But there are many other models (Hadot 2011: 102). In Hadot, P. (2011). *The Present Alone is Our Happiness. Conversations with Jeannie Carlier and Arnold I. Davidson*, translated by M. Djaballah and M. Chase, Stanford: Stanford University Press.

[34] 'When religious enthusiasm burns itself out, when mysteries no longer obfuscate problems, when faith cannot restrain the strongest minds, then moral and metaphysical questions can be posed again [....]. The strength of moral feeling that produced the [French] Revolution shows how religious feeling was too weak to prevent it [...]. The crowd was driven by a purely moral and social idea. This will probably happen again [...]. When religious beliefs are no longer strong enough to move people, they will increasingly turn to moral and then to the social ideas which will eventually predominate [...]' (Guyau 1878: 13).

utilitarianism of his time – would be a particularly strong tool in the human struggle against religious fears and mystified forms of authority:

> [W]hen facing religion, Epicureanism's force of resistance surpassed all other philosophies. As a matter of principle, Epicureanism rejected the miraculous and the supernatural… we can say that Epicurus and Lucretius embody the scientific and positivistic spirit of the modern utilitarians, which is why they remain strong (1878: 12).

Guyau explains that Epicureanism succeeded like no other philosophy in challenging religious ideas until the appearance of Christianity, which somehow triumphed over Epicurean materialism. According to Guyau, Epicureans 'were weak when they faced Christianity because they consistently emphasized our ultimate annihilation…[35] despite the fact that human beings desire to be immortal'.[36] Nevertheless, for Guyau, if Epicureanism was defeated, it was not destroyed. He says that 'after several centuries, when the enthusiasm for this new religion faded', *this* life in *this* earth were again found to have value and to be worth taking seriously.[37] Epicureanism re-emerges, therefore, with its attachment to the materiality of the earth,[38] and with it a contemporary Stoicism resumes the battle that defines the history of moral thought.

For Guyau, the interpretation of Epicurus could be also understood a *topos* for philosophical experimentation, in the sense of a territory to formulate his own concepts, and to examine the implications of a way of life. In order to illustrate this, we will focus on the specific interpretation Guyau provides of the Epicurean notion of pleasure [*plaisir*], showing what we believe is innovative about his reading and the conceptuality he mobilizes to explain this 'key idea' of

---

[35] For Nietzsche, this emphasis on mortality is one of the 'heroic' features of Epicureanism. In Vincenzo's perspective, Epicurus' denial of immortality 'affirms the most terrible character of existence as one of the first principles of the good life'. Also see Ansell-Pearson 2014: 25.

[36] The convergence with Nietzsche's account of the same process is striking. According to Lampert, 'Platonism triumphed over Epicureanism through the medium of Christianity but now, after modern science has reconquered the teaching of life after death in favour of the idea of 'definitive death', Nietzsche can say: 'And Epicurus triumphs anew!' (D §72)' (Lampert 1993: 425).

[37] 'As the centuries passed, human beings became tired of having their eyes restlessly turned to heaven [*le ciel*], and the earth [*la terre*] assumed a greater importance for everyone' (Guyau 1878: 13).

[38] Guyau speaks of a 'resurrection, both in France and England of the complete system of Epicureanism' (1878: 13).

Epicureanism. We would also like to show how Guyau, like Nietzsche in his middle works, finds in Epicurus a very important philosophical attitude, consisting of the attempt to restore to philosophy its claim to be an art of existence, to be a form of self-cultivation and a way of life.

The Epicurean Sage and the Art of Life

According to Guyau, pleasure is the principle (the 'key idea') of Epicureanism, characterizing the 'only end [*fin*] of desire' (35). Following Guyau's analysis, the enjoyment [*jouissance*] is good in itself and by itself, as well as all the means employed to achieve it. As Guyau explains, 'it is useless to examine the ways by which enjoyment is obtained', as well as the 'sequence of circumstances that lead to the *enjoyment* of pleasure' (36). In this regard, Epicurus' doctrine is similar to that of Aristippus and the Cyrenaic school.

Guyau reconstructs Aristippus' position as a form of radical hedonism, which could be synthesized through the idea of an absolute "fidelity" to the present moment, and consequently to the pleasure that is possible to achieve in each singular ephemeral fragment of the present. "Who knows what the future will be for us?" (p.36). For Aristippus, "the present alone is ours" (36). In this sense, we must subtract every thought involving duration and succession, making ourselves present to the actuality of enjoyment.

For Epicurus, we must consider pleasures and pains from the perspective of the whole of our lives (*ho hólos bíos*).[39] Passions, drives and desires appear to us as completely dominant when considered in the present. If we consider them in time and, specifically from the perspective of the duration of a whole life, we can then evaluate their ethical significance and ultimately master them. Guyau explains this idea through an analogy: *time* is for our *passions* what *space* is for *atoms*.[40] He says that as shocks and collisions of atoms are less violent and frequent in a vast space than they would be in a small space where atoms have less space to move freely; the same would be valid for our passions in the short and long term. When considered in the short span of the present they appear absolute and unconquerable. However, when pictured in the duration of our whole life, how violent and powerful can they actually be?

What is unique in Guyau's interpretation of Epicurus resides in the way he conceives the temporality of pleasure and happiness. While authors from Nietzsche to Hadot have highlighted the value of the *present instant* in

---

[40] Guyau 1878: 40.

Epicureanism,[41] Guyau shows that the recovery of the present moment, and the emphasis on the pleasure that can be found in the present, is *not* distinctive of Epicureanism. For Guyau, this distinctive character resides in a consideration of time that privileges the idea of the *future* when considering action in the present. Epicurean present must be traversed by the future, and both present and future converge in the composition of a 'whole of life'.[42] In Guyau's reconstruction, the introduction of the notion of temporality is concomitant with the appearance of the concept of the sage, the figure who incarnates the concept of Epicurean pleasure and the consideration of *ho hólos bíos*.[43] The sage is the moral agent that Epicureanism seeks to constitute; one which perhaps only Epicurus himself had fully embodied.

Pleasures and pains are viewed through the perspective of 'the whole duration of a life' (*ho hólos bíos*) and referred to a single *telos*, the achievement of happiness. The requirement for this achievement is that of coherence and consistence over time, and that is the existential decision of the sage. The Epicurean is not someone who indulges in undistinguishable pleasures – he is not the Cyrenaic hedonists who disperses themselves in a multitude of fleeting instants. The Epicurean sage is the one who chooses self-consistency over the chaos and contradiction of

---

[41] See for example Hadot and Nietzsche. Hadot understands the importance of the present as realisation of the spiritual exercise of meditation on death, which opens the perspective gratitude to the gift of existing. He quotes Horace's understanding of each particular moment is the product of chance, an unexpected gift, that we should accept with immense gratitude (Hadot 1995: 196). Similarly, for Nietzsche, according to Ansell-Pearson: 'For the middle period Nietzsche, Epicurus is the philosopher who affirms the moment, having neither resentment toward the past nor fear of the future' (Ansell-Pearson: 2013: 111). As Ansell-Pearson explains in a later article '[i]n Epicurus' teaching Nietzsche locates an appreciation of the moment' (Ansell-Pearson 2014a: 2).

[42] Undoubtedly, the present plays a key role in every hedonistic philosophy, but that is not the final word when it comes to Epicurus; in the same way, the future plays a key role in utilitarianism and in every form of utilitarian calculus, which according to Guyau is the compass that guides the Epicurean in the present.

[43] We could recall Kant's phrase according to which 'the pleasure of the Epicurean is the pleasure of the sage' (Ansell-Pearson 2014a: 14). On the other hand, it is possible to object that the Epicurean gods play this *exemplar* role which is more important than that of the sage. According to Hadot (1995: 190), the gods provide a vision of the 'model of wisdom', being the 'projection and incarnation of the Epicurean ideal of life', for their life consists in the enjoyment of their own perfection, of the pure pleasure of existing. See also Brun 1959: 93. See also Diogenes Laertius, X, 123; Lucretius, II, 646 – 651 and III, 14-24. Strodach identifies this role of the gods (2012: 40-43). The blessedness of the gods and the possibility of achieving a godly state among men is well expressed by Epicurus in the closing of his *Letter to Menoeceus*, 135.

desires and passions, directing his or her 'thought [and actions] towards the future', one who cultivates the whole of her or his life as a work of difficult and laborious elaboration, a work to which he strives to give a rational and beautiful form.

For the sage, each moment is filtered through the contact with the single end, making the sage's will concentrate and unitary, projecting itself beyond the present sensation. The present is thought through the future, which it helps to realize. Not a future life, but the future of *this* finite life,[44] which depends on the rational measuring of present pains and pleasures, a future which is up to us to shape according to the intelligent principle of happiness. The sage is the expression of the Epicurean idea according to which 'there is something superior to the present, a superior form of good which encompasses every particular good' (41). This is why when the sage chooses a present pleasure, he does so considering it as a part in the process of the constitution of an organized, rational, totality – that of a beautiful life.

In this sense, Guyau emphasizes an aesthetic aspect of Epicurus' moral philosophy. The unity and continuity in the axis of temporality – the production of a consistent way of life – could be understood as an ethical continuity of *style*. That is one of his points of contact with Nietzsche's middle-period works. In the *Gay Science*, Nietzsche says that '*One thing is needful* – to "give style" to one's character – a great and rare art!' (GS §290). Just like for Guyau's Epicurean sage, a single law, a single end and in Nietzsche's case a single 'taste' governs the creation of oneself through constant work and cultivation: 'In the end, when the work is finished, it becomes evident how the constraint of a single taste governed and formed everything large and small' (GS §290).

What does this beautiful style that one imposes to one's whole life consist in? Guyau says that for this work, beauty resides in harmony, that is, in a certain orderly relation of parts and whole, which connects the current instant and one's entire lifespan; between the modest pleasures one chooses to affirm and the pains that one chooses to endure as means for a greater, more stable and lasting delight with one's own existence. As Guyau explains:

> In the same way that Epicurus' conception [of pleasure] is greater and more complete than that of Aristippus, it is also more beautiful and yet more moral. From the aesthetic point of view, isn't there beauty in this rational disposition of life, in this subordination of the parts to the whole? (1878:42).

---

[44] This concern is shared with Nietzsche, who finds in Epicurus someone 'who teaches a new way of life by remaining true to the earth' (Ansell-Pearson 2014a: 4).

The sage is an 'artist of happiness' whose task is to organize rationally emotions and pleasures throughout his life in a whole in which parts have a specific position and connection. Guyau found in Epicurus what Foucault would identify in ancient ethics in the 1980s, the idea of an aesthetics of existence, an understanding of 'the *bios* as a material for an aesthetic piece of art' (Foucault 1994: 260). Similarly, Guyau uses the metaphor of the painter to define this 'artist of happiness' painting emotions, pleasures and pains on the picture [*cadre*] of life, placing them in different planes, with different importance in it. As Guyau says:

> Life then becomes this *cadre* of undetermined contours, in which the sage, this 'artist of happiness' [*artiste de bonheur*] groups his emotions to come, placing some of them in the second plane, some others in the first, bringing these to light, and casting the shadows of oblivion over the others.

The aesthetic value of the sage's life does not point to irrationality or any form of irrationalistic aestheticism, but on the contrary to the harmony and rationality that the sage is able to create throughout his life. The aesthetic value, the beauty of the work comes from this rational order, this intelligent organization of a lifestyle, in which certain pleasures are cultivated, aiming at a superior happiness.

Guyau finds in the sage what Nietzsche in his middle-period works also found in Epicureanism, an art of existence which takes the form of a refined asceticism.[45] In many ways this prefigures Nietzsche's view of the Hellenistic schools as 'experimental laboratories in which a considerable number of recipes for the art of living have been thoroughly practiced and lived to the hilt.'[46] For Guyau, the Epicurean recipe allows us to achieve a superlative form of pleasure by choosing less dangerous pleasures, which allows one to free oneself from the chaos and bondage to the passions. This form of blessedness is achieved in the contemplation of a coherent, consistent life oriented towards happiness. Unlike Guyau's view of the Cyrenaics, and similarly to Nietzsche's view of the task of giving style to one's character (GS §290), the Epicurean sage is able to exercise self-control, and the composition of his life as a coherent totality could be understood as a power to create '[self]constraint and perfection under a law of [his] own'. In this sense, Guyau's reading of Epicurus detaches pleasure from

---

[45] Ansell-Pearson, 2014a: 4. Roos, 2000: 298.
[46] Nietzsche, KSA 9, 15 [59]. Cited by Hadot 2002: 277 and 2011: 102. See also Ansell-Pearson 2014: 240 for Nietzsche's account of the 'modern conditions' affecting how such 'recipes for the art of living' are implemented.

indulgent hedonism, integrating it into a whole economy of life by way of virtues and practices of self-cultivation. We claim that Guyau's appropriation of the Epicurean art of living presages Foucault account of Greek ethics as a 'care of the self' in which the ancients 'had a *tekhne tou biou* in which the economy of pleasure played a very large role. In this "art of life" the notion of exercising a perfect mastery on oneself soon became the main issue' (Foucault 1986: 259).

Works Cited

Works by Jean-Marie Guyau

Guyau, J-M. (1875). *Etude sur la Philosophie d'Épictète et traduction du Manuel d'Épictète*. Paris: Delagrave.

—(1878). *La morale d'Épicure et ses rapports avec les doctrines contemporaines*. Paris: Germer Baillière et Cie.

—(1879). *La morale anglaise contemporaine*. Paris: Germer Baillière et Cie.

—(1881). *Vers d'un philosophe*. Paris: Germer Baillière et Cie.

—(1884). *Les problèmes de l'esthétique contemporaine*. Paris: Félix Alcan.

—(2012a) [1885]. *Esquisse d'une morale sans obligation ni sanction. Mit den Annotationen von Friedrich Nietzsche: Rekonstruktion der kritischen Lektüre von Friedrich Nietzsche mit Marginalien*, Ilse Walther-Dulk (ed.). Weimar.

—(2012b). *Esquisse d'une morale sans obligation ni sanction: avec les textes de Nietzsche et Kropotkine*. Biographie, préface, postface de Jordi Riba; Note polémique de Louis Janover. Paris: Payot et Rivages

—(1887). *L'irréligion de l'avenir: Etude sociologique*. Paris: Félix Alcan.

—(1888). *L'art au point de vue sociologique*. Paris: Félix Alcan.

—(1889). *Éducation et hérédité: Etude sociologique*. Paris: Félix Alcan. [Posthumously published; edited by A. Fouillée].

—(1890). *La genèse de l'idée de temps*. Paris: Félix Alcan. [Posthumously published; edited by A. Fouillée].

—(2010). *A gênese da idéia de tempo e outros ensaios*. Trans. R. Schöpke & M. Baladi. São Paulo: Martins Fontes.

Critical Notices and Reviews

Bergson, H. (1891). 'Analyse de l'ouvrage: J.-M. Guyau *La genèse de l'idée de temps avec une introduction par Albert Fouillée*'. *Revue philosophique*, *31*, 185–190.

Boirac, E. (1878). 'Analyse de l'ouvrage: J.-M. Guyau, *La morale d'Épicure et ses rapports avec les doctrines contemporaines*'. *Revue philosophique*, *6*, 513–522 and 646–648.

—(1879). 'Analyse de l'ouvrage: J.-M. Guyau, *La morale anglaise contemporaine: Morale de l'utilité et de l'évolution*, *Revue philosophique*, *8*, 411–425.

Sidgwick, H. (1879). 'Review: J.-M. Guyau *La morale d'Épicure et ses rapports avec les doctrines contemporaines*'. *Mind* IV (16): 582–587.

Sully, J. (1890). 'Review: J.-M. Guyau, *L'art au point de vue sociologique*. And *Éducation et hérédité: Etude sociologique*.' *Mind* XV (58): 279–284.

Whittaker, T. (1889). 'Review: A. Fouillée, *La morale, l'art et la religion d'après Guyau*. *Mind* XIV (54): 295–296.

Works by Other Authors

Archambault, P. (1911). *Guyau*. Paris: Librairie Bloud & Cie.

Bergmann, E. (1912). *Die Philosophie Guyaus*. Leipzig: Verlag Dr. W. Klinkhardt.

Bergson, H. (1889). *Time and free will*. New York: Macmillan.

Brun, J. (1959). *L'épicurisme*. Paris: PUF.

Dauriac, L. (1890). Philosophes contemporains: M. Guyau. *Année philosophique*, 1, 222. Diogenes Laertius (1931). *Lives of Emienent Philosophers*. Trans. R.D. Hicks. London & Cambridge : Harvard University Press.

Didi-Huberman, G. (2000). *Devant le temps: Histoire de l'art et anachronisme des images.*Paris : Les Éditions de Minuit..

Durkheim, E. (1887). 'Guyau: L'irreligion de l'avenir, étude de sociologie', *Revue Philosophique* XXIII.

Epicurus (2012). *The Art of Happiness*. Trans. G.K. Strodach. London : Penguin.

Epicure (2011). *Lettres, maximes et autres textes*. Trans. Pierre-Marie Morel. Paris : Flammarion.

Fouillée, A. (1895). *Pages choisis des grand écrivains: J.-M. Guyau*. Paris: Armand Colin and Cie.

—(1889). *La morale, l'art et la religion d'après Guyau*. Paris: Félix Alcan.

—(1902). 'The Ethics of Nietzsche and Guyau'. *International Journal of Ethics*, Vol.13, no.1, 13-27.

Foucault, M. (1984) [1986]. *History of Sexuality: The Care of the Self*, translated by R. Hurley, London, Penguin.

—(1994) [1982]. *Ethics*, P. Rabinow (ed.), translated by R. Hurley and others. Penguin Books.

Guyau, A. (1913). *La philosophie et la sociologie d'Alfred Fouillée*. Paris: Félix Alcan.

Hadot, P. (2011). *The Present Alone is Our Happiness*. Conversations with Jeannie Carlier and Arnold I. Davidson, translated by M. Djaballah and M. Chase, Stanford: Stanford University Press.

—(1995). *Qu'est-ce que la philosophie antique?* Paris : Gallimard.

Høffding, H. (1894). *Den nyere Filosofis Historie*. Copenhagen: Gyldendal.Knight, A.H.J. (1933).

Lucretius (2007). *The Nature of Things*. Trans. A.E. Stallings; Intro. R. Jenkyns. London: Penguin.

Nietzsche, F. (1974) [1882]. *The Gay Science*, trans. W. Kaufmann. Vintage.

Nussbaum, M. (1994). "Pity and Mercy: Nietzsche's Stoicism," in *Nietzsche, Genealogy, Morality: Essays on Nietzsche's Genealogy of Morals*, Richard Schacht (ed.) University of California Press.

Pfeil, H. (1928). *Jean-Marie Guyau und die Philosophie des Lebens*. Augsburg: Dr. Benno Filser Verlag.

Recent Scholarship

Ansell-Pearson, K. (2009). 'Free spirits and free thinkers: Nietzsche and Guyau on the Future of Morality.' In Jeffrey A. Metzger (ed.), *Nietzsche, Nihilism, and the Philosophy of the Future*. Continuum, 102–124.

—(2013), 'True to the Earth: Nietzsche's Epicurean Care of Self and World', in Hutter, H. and Friedland, E. (eds.), *Nietzsche's Therapeutic Teaching For Individuals and Culture*. Bloomsbury.

—(2014a). 'Heroic-Idyllic Philosophizing: Nietzsche and the Epicurean Tradition'. *Royal Institute of Philosophy Supplements*. 74 . pp. 237-263.

—(2014b). 'Contra Kant and Beyond Nietzsche: Naturalizing Ethics in the Work of Jean-Marie Guyau', *Hegel Bulletin*, 35. pp. 185-203.

—(2015). 'Beyond Obligation? Jean-Marie Guyau on Life and Ethics'. *Royal Institute of Philosophy Supplement*, 77: 207–225.

—(2015). Beyond Selfishness: Epicurean Ethics in Nietzsche and Guyau. In Bamford, R. , (ed.) Nietzsche's Free Spirit Philosophy. Rowman & Littlefield International, pp. 49-69.

Lampert, L. (1993). *Nietzsche and Modern Times: A Study of Bacon, Descartes, and Nietzsche*. New Haven: Yale University Press.

Ricoeur, P. (1988). 'From Kant to Guyau'. In J. A. Michon, V. Pouthas & J. L. Jackson (Eds.), *Guyau and the idea of time* (pp. 149–159). Amsterdam: KNAW.

Roos, R. (2000). 'Nietzsche et Épicure: l'idylle héroïque,' in Jean-François Balaudé and Patrick Wotling (eds.), Lectures de Nietzsche. Paris: Librairie Générale Française, pp. 283–350

Testa, F. (2011). 'A arte do ponto de vista sociológico: a estética e a sociologia menor de Jean-Marie Guyau', *Cultura e Fé: Revista de Humanidades*, v. 34, n. 132, pp. 41-56

Ure, M. (2008) *Nietzsche's Therapy: Self-Cultivation in the Middle Period Works*. Lexington Books.

—(2009) 'Nietzsche's Free Spirit Trilogy and Stoic Therapy', *Journal of Nietzsche Studies*, 38.1, pp. 60–84.

Vincenzo, J. (1994). 'Nietzsche and Epicurus', *Man and World*, 27.4, p. 383–397.

Introduction[1]
Epicureanism in Antiquity and Modernity

Jean-Marie Guyau

[§1][p.9][2] The ethics of [self]interest [*morale de l'intérêt*], espoused for a hundred years by many French thinkers and today by the main English philosophers, is not such a historical novelty. We know that a similar doctrine, under the name of Epicureanism, seduced antiquity. It was the most popular philosophy of Greece and Rome. "The disciples and friends of Epicurus are so many," wrote Diogenes Laertius, "that whole towns would not be sufficient to contain them."[3] Plutarch claims that Epicurus's followers came from as far as Egypt to listen to their master and erected bronze statues in his honour.

Later, when the Romans began a relationship with the culture of the Greek people, they were still full of their own religious beliefs, uniting the love for their fatherland and cult of Jupiter Capitoline in their hearts. [However,] the essentially irreligious doctrine of Epicurus was the first [Greek] doctrine to enter Rome, and the [p.10] first to be expressed in the Latin language.

---

[1] Translated by Federico Testa with the editorial assistance of Matthew Dennis. Irene Dal Poz collaborated in the work with Guyau's classical references, sources and footnotes.

[2] The translator introduced this paragraph system in order to make possible to easily identify the passages in the French original. The original pagination from 1878 is kept in square brackets.

[3] Diogenes Laertius, *Lives of Eminent Philosophers* Book X, Section 9. Guyau adds "disciples" which does not appear in the Greek text. See R. D. Hicks: "his friends, so many in number that they could hardly be counted by whole cities".

Epicureanism had more than enough strength to defeat this ancient [Roman] religion immediately.[4] As Cicero notes "the multitude had its interest stirred, and flocked around Epicurus' system in preference to any other".[5] "Not only in Greece and Italy," he tells us, but "even the barbaric world has been stirred by Epicurus' thought"[6]. He tells us that "the people is with them", referring to the Epicureans.[7]

Indeed, most of the educated men were already with the Epicureans, and did remain with them for a long time. Their adversaries, the Stoics, struggled in vain against the Epicureans and this struggle lasted for the duration of the Roman Empire. The Stoics, however, could neither weaken nor defeat them, nor could they escape their influence. Seneca strongly criticised the Epicureans, although he was still nourished by [the thought of] Epicurus, who he admires and frequently quotes. He was attracted to the very doctrines he fought against. Epictetus later took up the fight against the Epicureans, railing against them with extreme violence. But his disciple, Marcus Aurelius, while having the same ideas and beliefs as Epictetus, returned to Epicurus, taking him as a model and exhorting himself to imitate him [Epicurus] without regret. Furthermore, he established a *chaire* of Epicureanism in Athens. Here and there in his meditations, which he so sincerely expressed, one recognises the great Epicurean conceptions, as if vaguely floating in a dream. Constantly and disquietly, Marcus Aurelius finds Epicureanism within his own ideas, and although he confronts it, his last thought [on Epicurean ideas] would be haunted by doubt. Lucian, a man determined to

---

[4] See M. Tullius Cicero, *Tusculanae Disputationes*, Book IV; *Academica*, Book I, Section 2; *Epistulae ad Familiares*, Book XV, 19. The first philosophical writers in Rome where the Epicureans Amafinius, Rabirius, and Catius – extremely mediocre writers, according to Cicero. The great poet and philosopher Lucretius appears after them.

[5] *Tusculanae Disputationes*, IV, 3. *T.N.* Here, the translation choice was to keep Guyau's phrasing. The original and extended quote is "To fill the gap their silence left came the voice of C. Amafinius, and by the publication of his works the crowd had its interest stirred, and flocked to the teaching he advocated in preference to any other, whether because it was so easy to grasp, or because of the seductive allurements of pleasure, or possibly also because, in the absence of any better teaching, they clung to what there was."

[6] *De Finibus Bonorum et Malorum*, Book II, Section XV.

[7] *De Finibus Bonorum et Malorum*, Book II, Section XIV. "himself and his friends [Epicureans] there have been so many later champions of his theory, which somehow or other enlists the support of that least competent but most powerful adherent, the general public."

doubt [*douteur resolu*], who typically does not spare philosophers from his mockery and fierce blows [*coups de bâton*], talks of Epicurus as a [p.11] "divine man, a saint, the only one to have known the truth, who, by communicating it to his disciples, became their liberator [*libérateur*]".[8]

[§2] Even at this time, after five centuries of struggle we can see that Epicureanism had not lost its importance. The sacred aura [*auréole*] with which the Epicureans ensconced [*entourer*] their master had not faded.

[§3] Epicurus' doctrine survived as long as paganism. Epicureanism remained standing, even when new beliefs emerged in the world. In the face of nascent Christianity, for example, Epicureanism remained as a constant temptation. Even Saint Augustine, who personifies the Christian epoch, admits that he would be inclined [*pendre*] towards Epicureanism.[9]

[§4] Indeed, when facing religion, Epicureanism's force of resistance surpassed all other philosophies. As a matter of principle, Epicureanism rejected the miraculous [*merveilleux*] and the supernatural. In fact, [we can say that] Epicurus and Lucretius already embody the scientific and positivistic spirit of the modern utilitarians, which is why they remain strong. The practical weakness of Epicureanism, when facing Christianity, was the persistence with which they emphasised our ultimate annihilation and the reality of our death. Human beings, however, desire to be immortal. At this time, people were weary of life, overwhelmed by servitude and decadence. Saint Augustine rejects [*repoussa*] a doctrine that promised him nothing more than a happy life [*vie heureuse*], as did his era. Gradually the *gardens of Epicurus*,[10] where previously sages of every nation had

---

[8] Lucian, *Alexander*, 61. Guyau's translation is shorter, for he abbreviates the Greek original text. The original reads: "Epicurus, a man truly saintly and divine in his nature, who alone truly discerned right ideals and handed them down, who proved himself the liberator of all who sought his converse".

[9] *Confessions*, Book VI, XXVI, "I used to argue with my friends Alypius and Nebridius about the limits of good and evil. Had I not believed that the soul, and the rewards we have deserved, persist after death, which Epicurus did not, I would have given the victory in my mind to Epicurus. Moreover, I used to ask, if we were immortal and lived in perpetual pleasures of the flesh with no fear of being deprived, why were we not happy?" Thus, it was simply time that separated Epicurus from Saint Augustine. Guyau indicates the wrong reference.

[10] Italic in the original.

wandered tranquilly, which had been surrounded by an enchanted crowd of followers, became deserted for centuries. [p.12] The words of the pagan master, words that each disciple learned by heart and committed to his soul as sacred truth, were forgotten and effaced by more powerful words. Humankind, then, faced a new future, and ascended the mountain where an attainable view of heaven was shown and the doctrine of a 'single God' [*un Dieu*] was preached.

[§5] Epicureanism was defeated; however, it was not destroyed. After several centuries, when the enthusiasm for this new religion faded, when believers dwindled and its thinkers became less numerous, it was discovered that earthly interests walked hand in hand with celestial ones. The earth was found to have value and to be worth taking seriously. As the centuries passed, human beings became tired of having their eyes restlessly turned to heaven [*le ciel*]; the earth [*la terre*] assumed a greater importance for everyone. Montaigne clearly represents this transition. He was not an Epicurean, but a Pyrrhonian. What is convenient about Pyrrhonism is that one can be Pyrrhonian while simultaneously being many other things. Scepticism does not exclude anything, precisely because it rejects everything. But it only rejects everything in theory. In practice it acknowledges something, and Pyrrhonism acknowledged only that which it wished to acknowledge. A Sceptic may get along with everyone by following all dominant beliefs and, nevertheless, he can be free with everyone [*avec tout le monde*]. An Epicurean, on the contrary, cannot be other than Epicurean – and he is an enemy to everyone who is not. Thus Montaigne would push this despised [*peu aimé*] sobriquet ['Epicurean'] away from him. But in fact he will not be any less an Epicurean disciple than a Pyrrhonian one. How many Epicurean thoughts are reborn in Montaigne, infiltrating his wavering [*ondoyant*] book, *The Essays*! After one hundred years, Montaigne's century was nourished by his writings and generations meditated on his book. This "handbook of the honest" – as it was called by a priest – it is not the scepticism of Pyrrho that will come out of this meditation, but rather the *ethics* [*morale*] of Epicurus.

[§6] Around the first half of the seventeenth century saw [p.13] the resurrection in both France and England of the complete system of Epicureanism. In France, it was reawakened by the cautious erudition of Gassendi; in England, it was reawakened by the rigorous genius of Hobbes. From this moment onwards, Epicurean ideas recovered their place in history, and their supporters become as numerous as they once were. Even such a misanthropic and dark thinker as La Rochefoucauld – a thinker who only seems to care for the finesses and curiosities of psychological analysis – is lead towards Epicurus unwittingly. Combined with

Spinozist naturalism, it is Epicureanism that is born again with Helvétius, d'Holbach, Saint-Lambert. It is Epicureanism that inspires all the French writers of the eighteenth century (excluding Montesquieu, Turgot and Rousseau). Then Epicureanism returns in England, gathering in Hobbes' homeland ever more numerous *partisans*. With Bentham and Mill it assumes its definitive form which, as we will see, does not differ much from its original source. Finally, with Spencer and Darwin it grows anew. To the more or less transformed moral system of Epicurus is added a wide cosmological system: new Democritians provide modern Epicureans with the means to ground their ethics in the laws of the whole universe, encompassing man and the universe in the same conception.

[§7] To summarise, Epicureanism, so powerful in antiquity, has returned to dominate two of the greatest nations of Europe. In France, it is crucial for Helvétius and almost all eighteenth-century French philosophers; in England, it is crucial for Bentham and the contemporary English school. Today almost all English thinkers are Epicurean. Furthermore, Epicurus' influence in our country [France], which has remained considerable since the last century, is increasing despite the new Stoicism of Kant and his school. Everywhere, in theory and in practice, [p.14] we find two moralities [*morales*], which assume two opposing understandings [*conceptions*] of the visible and invisible world. These two doctrines split philosophical thought and divide human beings. We could say that today the fierce half-a-millennium struggle between the Epicureans and Stoics has rekindled and is burning anew.

[§8] This battle between moral doctrines, which follows the laws of thought, tends to increasingly occupy our minds. Indeed, if there is something that interests the whole of humanity, if there is something that makes us passionate, it is the problem of morality [*le problème moral*]. No human being's attention fails to be captured when they hear of 'duty', 'justice', or 'rights'. Only one thing could have diverted attention from moral and social issues during a whole historical epoch: religious enthusiasm. Religious faith satisfies both human tendencies: to be disinterested and to be utilitarian.[11] The tendency to be disinterested takes divine love as its object and suffuses this with human love. The utilitarian tendency [*l'intérêt*] [*viz.* the tendency to be self-interested] defers its satisfaction by anticipating a future [*l'attente*] in which all believed. To a certain extent, the self-interested could defer their satisfaction of the good things of the earth by anticipating the joy of heaven. Each time a religion triumphs it flattens

---

[11] *T.N.* Guyau uses the French *utilitaire*, designating self-interested moral behaviour.

philosophical and moral discussions, spreading indifference to worldly duties and rights. When religious enthusiasm burns itself out, when mysteries (accepted until then and projected as immense shadows upon the human mind)[12] no longer obfuscate problems, when faith cannot restrain the strongest minds, then moral and metaphysical questions can be posed again. Only when attention turns from temples and heaven to moral and political philosophy, only when prophets and soothsayers are forgotten, do the people gather around thinkers who strive to show them what is present and real.

[p.15] Nevertheless, the eighteenth and nineteenth centuries manifest this kind of crisis. Those with a strong faith appear to be decreasing, and even those who still have enthusiasm in faith no longer have it with the same intensity. This occurs in all nations, although it is especially widespread in France, which was shown by the French Revolution. We could say that the strength of moral sentiment that produced the Revolution shows how religious feeling was too weak to prevent it. It is a unique historical example of a great movement in which religious feeling did not play a role. The crowd was driven by a purely moral and social idea. This will undoubtedly happen again. Humanity is always the same, which is to say easy to impassion. It was dragged forward by an idea. When religious beliefs are no longer strong enough to move people, they will increasingly turn to moral and then to the social ideas, which will eventually predominate and absorb everything including morals.

[§9] We can say, therefore, that moral and social issues will become alive [*vivantes*]. They will not be limited to the abstract domain of philosophical thought, but will pass into the realm of fact and action. They will become matters of life and death for us. Those nations that had too viciously tackled religious problems were often outdated and surpassed [*effaces*] by those who offered a less imperfect solution. Religious sentiment always gave the nations in which it manifested at a high level the force to expand. This will happen in the future with moral or social feelings. Those who understand sociality more accurately will have an irresistible power far ahead of others. [p.16] The best solution to moral and social problems will be the strength of the people who find this solution.

[§10] Now, what is the people and who is the person who will get closest to finding the solution, or that will at least be able to approach it? If it was possible

---

[12] *T.N.* Parentheses were added in order to separate clauses which are part of a same long sentence in Guyau's original.

JEAN-MARIE GUYAU

to predict the future, to determine how events will unfold, then the one who knew these moral and social truths could impose a direction on history, just as one can set the course of a ship when one knows where it is heading. But we no longer live in times in which one affirmed with priestly certainty where the truth lies. Absolute certainty in the correctness of one's own thought is [one idea] of the same variety as religious ideas, and it is doomed to become weak like they do.

We are now less willing to believe, more willing to search. We defy our own thinking. We saw so many ideas crumble around us, and sometimes even our own, so we no longer dare to rely on ourselves with complete confidence. Whatever we assert we are always still doubtful, and are ready to restrict our assertions. Is this bad? No, because circumspection does not prevent the fierce drive to research. If we are to discover the truth, we must be tireless in our pursuit of it.

[§11] If this fierce drive to pursue the truth possesses us, it is especially when it pertains to problems that are connected to the behaviour of individuals and societies. It is a kind of duty to research whose side duty is on and on whose side humanity must go. The whole moral and social debate, which we have seen growing in importance, can be reduced to the debate between the partisans of [self]interestedness [*l'intérêt*] or the partisans of meritorious virtue [*vertu méritoire*], between the Epicureans and their detractors. Does duty exist? Does morality exist? Are we worthy to do what we think is good? Or rather, "duty", "morality", "worthiness", are these just [p.17] (as there are many reasons to believe) figurative expressions that humanity has taken too literally? Must we replace "duty" by "common interest", "morality" by "instinct" or by "hereditary habit" or "calculation"? Must we replace "merit" in action by the "enjoyment" [*jouissance*] of acting? Essentially, this is the very same issue broached by Epicurus, whose thought now echoes in today's greatest minds and which answers our questions. We already know enough about Epicurean morality, and its subsequent development in history, to understand the strength of his system. Most often, the strength or weakness of a philosophical doctrine can be measured by its duration, its persistence. Part of humanity has believed that life's sole purpose was [self]interest. Part of humanity believed this and still supports it. If this is not the whole truth, at least it is a large part of the whole truth. Such a doctrine therefore deserves the most careful consideration.

[§12] Doctrines have their own life, like individuals. They are born, they grow, they flourish. They blossom in their youth and they mature with virile vigour. They also decline sometimes – but not always – and there are some that are

109

immortal. In order to know a doctrine is good to have somehow followed in its path, seen its progress, to have lived by it. How could we expect to know those [doctrines] which we only see *en passant,* fleetingly, in only one aspect? When we see Epicureanism unwound before us in its entirety, in all its many guises, only then can we know, or even hope to know, what is true or false in it. Only then we can also try to judge it – judgment will never be without appeal – because a doctrine has always the future in front of it to rise up if necessary, and neither the history nor the critique of systems are ever finished.

Book Reviews

Nietzsche's Philosophy of History—Anthony Jensen
(Cambridge, UK: Cambridge University Press, pp. 250, 2013. ISBN: 978-1-10-702732-9)

Jennifer O. Gammage

Anthony K. Jensen's *Nietzsche's Philosophy of History* is a welcome treatment of an under-appreciated aspect of one of Nietzsche's most influential philosophical contributions. Despite the title, Jensen's painstakingly researched account could just as easily be considered a history *of* Nietzsche's philosophy. Although Jensen is primarily writing from and for the Anglo-American tradition of scholarship, his historical research makes this book helpful for a Nietzsche scholar of any school. The book follows a chronological trajectory, tracing the development of Nietzsche's meta-historical thought from his philological writings through *Ecce Homo*, ultimately culminating in his positive contribution to the philosophy of history: Nietzsche's mature conceptions of what Jensen refers to as his perspectival theory of explanation and representational anti-realist position of description and justification.

Jensen's first chapter analyzes Nietzsche's early philological works to argue that he started out as an ontological and representational realist employing naturalist, psychological models of explanation to account for discrepancies of record. Jensen argues that Nietzsche is committed to ontological and representation realism in all of his early works. For early Nietzsche, the philologist or historian can accurately represent past events as they actually happened. Jensen will go on to argue that Nietzsche later lets go of his representational realism while retaining his ontological realism, but in this chapter and the one that follows he claims that Nietzsche's early meta-historical views were not so radical. In fact, according to Jensen, Nietzsche's appeal to psychological factors retains a sober naturalism in contrast to his contemporaries, who employed supernatural mechanisms as historical drivers. In highlighting Nietzsche's appeal to psychological motivations such as hate, jealousy, fear, and the need for recognition, Jensen does a fine job bringing out the ways in which his early work already foreshadows his later genealogical work.

Jensen's second chapter dives more deeply into the historical context of Nietzsche's days as a student and philologist, situating him within the debate between his two teachers, Ritschl (a student of Hermann's *Sprachphilologie*, with its emphasis on verifiability and rigor) and Jahn (a student of Boeckh's *Sachphilologie*, with its emphasis on the pedagogical power of research into antiquity). What is most striking about Jensen's work here is his refusal to neatly locate either Ritschl or Jahn too rigidly within the camps of their mentors. Instead, he offers a more robust and careful analysis of the ways in which Nietzsche inherited an approach that blends strict method with hermeneutic and humanistic focuses from these mentors. Jensen determines that Nietzsche's break with Ritschl and Jahn was not so much based on a disagreement of method as it was a rupture between world-views. Although this claim is somewhat confusing given Jensen's formulation of Nietzsche's split with Ritschl and Jahn — as one in which Schopenhauer's idealistic metaphysics won out over Ritschl's empiricism and Wagner's aristocratic artist won out over Jahn's democratic ideals of enlightenment — Jensen's claim that the dispute was not a methodological one merits recognition insofar as it warns against any easy interpretation of Nietzsche's ambivalence regarding philology and philosophy.

In chapter three, Jensen makes an original argument in which he rejects any attempt to see *Birth of Tragedy* as continuous with Nietzsche's contiguous works. Instead, Jensen frames Nietzsche's treatment of tragedy as a sudden break with prominent philological and historiographical methodologies of his time, a break he would soon denounce. Much of this chapter is spent developing a very clear and compelling account of Schopenhauer's aesthetic intuition (*Anschauung*). Jensen argues that Nietzsche's account of Greek tragedy breaks with his other writings insofar as it offers supernatural explanations and relies upon a Schopenhaurian notion of objectivity. Because Jensen sees Nietzsche holding onto both ontological and representational realism in this work, he reads Nietzsche as making objective claims that are grounded in aesthetic intuition, which breaks through the subject-object dichotomy to perceive pure ideas without mediation. This is a problem for Nietzsche because it shows an internal inconsistency: Nietzsche's account claims objective status but is not verifiable. While Jensen's account of aesthetic intuition is helpful for understanding some of what Nietzsche is up to in the *Birth of Tragedy*, Jensen's argument would benefit from additional support here. Why should we think Nietzsche wanted to provide a timeless account of the essence of Greek tragedy when he gives an account of tragedy that shows it developing from the interplay of historical forces? And if he did not, why would we assume Nietzsche is holding as tightly to representational realism in his first book as Jensen assumes?

The next two chapters lay out Nietzsche's mature meta-historical position, first in terms of Nietzsche's critiques of scientistic and teleological historiography and in terms of Nietzsche's positive account. Nietzsche's critiques of "historical sense" should be familiar to his readers, and Jensen's reconstruction provides rich details that place Nietzsche in dialogue with his predecessors and contemporaries. In the fifth chapter, Jensen explicitly argues for what he takes to be Nietzsche's own position, which Jensen charts along three axes: description, explanation, and objectivity.

Jensen here employs a two-step argument aimed at showing that Nietzsche is an anti-realist regarding descriptive and explanatory representation. Drawing primarily upon Nietzsche's "Truth and Lies…" essay, Jensen argues that the mature Nietzsche thinks historical events are too complex to be properly communicated, understood, or recorded. Because our language is only ever an approximation of the effects of the material world on our sense organs, we cannot use it to describe reality as it is. Furthermore, since reality is more complex than the impressions it makes upon us, it is too complex to be recorded or causally tracked. Thus, Nietzsche cannot be a realist about representation, and the historian cannot hope to offer an account that corresponds directly to historical events. These ontological and epistemological claims commit the mature Nietzsche to an anti-realist view of representation at the level of explanation as well. If reality is more complex than we can properly perceive, then we also cannot derive general laws or causal structures from particular historical events. Our explanations of historical events and processes will always reveal our particular, historical, and perspectival interpretations.

To save this position from accusations of relativism, Jensen insists upon a Nietzschean notion of objectivity. The thrust of Jensen's argument is that Nietzsche maintains a criterion of consensus among like types. While subjects might be singular for Nietzsche, they nevertheless have physiological drives and willed aims in common. Moreover, because the historian is historically situated in a shared world, she will also be situated within a community that shares a framework for making sense of the world at the level of language and institutions. Jensen appeals to consensus among like types living in a shared sphere of meaning as the criterion of objectivity that keeps Nietzsche from sliding into the sort of full-blown relativism that would make him irrelevant to philosophy of history.

While Jensen's argument for objectivity is laudable insofar as he moves deftly between very difficult and dynamic aspects of Nietzsche's thought and manages to hold his footing while doing so, it would take more to make his claims ultimately convincing. Jensen appears to ascribe the democratic ideal of stable consensus to Nietzsche, which is at odds with Nietzsche's condemnation of "herd mentality" and insistence on perpetual "overcoming." At times, Jensen appeals to the criterion of "health" in order to show that Nietzsche gives us a way to differentiate between conflicting historical accounts (based on their ability to serve life and the flourishing of will to power), and here the argument is more promising. Still it is unclear why we would want to call this "objectivity." There are surely ways to distinguish perspectivism from relativism that do not require us to hold so tightly to terms Nietzsche seems to eschew.

Jensen's last two chapters show the position he sketches in chapter five at work in the *Genealogy* and *Ecce Homo*. His reading of the former focuses on the concept of emergence to highlight contingency and the necessity of conflict between competing historical accounts, while also distinguishing perspectivism from postmodern approaches. His reading of the latter rejects attempts to dismiss Nietzsche's autobiographical work or align it with contemporary standpoint epistemologies. Jensen does this by stressing Nietzsche's ontological realism even within the context of an ontology of a self that is always in progress, engaged in dynamic and mutually constitutive interactions with a world that is itself fluid. Jensen's reading of *Ecce Homo* is inspired and nicely articulates much of what makes Nietzsche's account of history indispensable for his vision of will to power. Despite the fact that Jensen seems invested in maintaining the subject-object split in the post-*Birth* works, the force of his reading suggests that this dichotomy is undermined by Nietzsche's ontological project. This is worth taking seriously, not only to do justice to Nietzsche's own thinking, but also to more thoroughly understand some possible implications of retaining objectivity alongside Nietzsche's perspectivism.

Nietzsche Versus Paul—Abed Azzam

(New York, NY: Columbia University Press, pp. 209, 2015. ISBN 978-0-231-16930-1)

Joseph M. Spencer

In a 1974 essay, Jörg Salaquarda provided an illuminating preliminary analysis of the occasional claim that Nietzsche's "vehemence" in his polemic against Saint Paul is symptomatic of a certain "closeness" or "kinship" between the two figures (102). According to Salaquarda, Nietzsche and Paul are in fact best read as rival revaluators, parallel in structure if nonetheless opposed in content: Paul is the teacher of the destruction of the (Jewish) law, Nietzsche the teacher of eternal recurrence (128). Whatever the merits of Salaquarda's conclusions, however, the importance of such an interpretation of Nietzsche has often been less than apparent—of interest, perhaps, only to those who might for reasons of faith wish to defend Paul against his critics. But thanks to the past two decades, which have witnessed a remarkable and unanticipated surge of interest in the philosophical significance of Saint Paul, the relevance of Salaquarda's question is now plain. Indeed, in the work that arguably inaugurated the shift in philosophical interest toward the Christian apostle—Alain Badiou's *Saint Paul*—there appears a brief argument that "Nietzsche is Paul's rival far more than his opponent" (72). The validity of such a claim deserves renewed critical attention. In *Nietzsche Versus Paul*, Abed Azzam begins to fill this need.

It is to be hoped, however, that the occasion for Azzam's book does not overdetermine its reception, as it certainly promises to do. Titled *Nietzsche Versus Paul* and lacking any clarifying subtitle, the book will likely draw the attention primarily of those interested in Paul's relationship to philosophy. But Azzam's intentions drastically outstrip any desire just to contribute to the conversation surrounding Paul. Indeed, *Nietzsche Versus Paul* is, unlike the best contributions to philosophical work on Paul, little interested in clarifying or developing the meaning or philosophical implications of Paul's own texts, on their own terms. Azzam seeks primarily—if not solely—to clarify the significance, *for Nietzsche and for the task of interpreting Nietzsche*, of Nietzsche's interactions with Paul. There is no attempt to decide on whether Nietzsche understands Paul correctly, nor is there any attempt at a defense of Pauline ideas against Nietzsche's critiques. Only seldom does Azzam draw on Pauline ideas or texts that do not explicitly appear in Nietzsche's writings. For Azzam, then, it seems it is largely enough just to make clear what Nietzsche means to say about Paul.

This is not to say, however, that Azzam's aims in the book are modest. *Nietzsche Versus Paul* is not a simple exegetical study, systematically working through Nietzsche's scattered references to and occasional sustained engagements with Paul. Although it in fact does provide exegeses of Nietzsche's many discussions of Paul (and of Christianity generally), it is primarily a thesis-driven attempt at a full reinterpretation of Nietzsche's larger project. Azzam in fact takes as his framing interlocutors Martin Heidegger and Gilles Deleuze, two overdetermined philosophical interpreters of Nietzsche's *oeuvre*. Like them, Azzam aims at excavating "the essential-Nietzsche" (xiii), but he criticizes Heidegger and Deleuze for having wrongly delimited themselves to "the horizon of the history of philosophy," that is, for presenting Nietzsche as exhausted by his opposition to Plato (147). Against these interpretations, Azzam presents an "essential-Nietzsche" who is more anti-*Christ* than anti-*Plato*. That is, Azzam's Nietzsche is chiefly a genealogical critic of (Pauline) Christianity who looks to the possible reemergence of the Dionysian, rather than a philosophical opponent of Plato who merely sees Christianity as a pitiful and problematic popularization of Platonism. In short, Azzam takes seriously and provides an extended study of Nietzsche's late formula, "Dionysus versus the Crucified."

Azzam's argument—which he explicitly presents as a furthering of Salaquarda's "inspiring" analysis (xvi)—unfolds over the course of six chapters. Each pair of two conjoined chapters focuses on a different historical period in Nietzsche's genealogical interpretation of the West. Chapter One addresses pre-Christian Greek developments from the rise of Dionysian religion to mature (but still pre-Christian) Platonism, while Chapter Two turns to pre-Christian Judaism both in what Nietzsche calls its noble, earlier form and in what he calls its priestly, later form. Chapter Three then focuses on the extra-historical figure of Jesus, Nietzsche's Buddhist idiot, before Chapter Four assesses Saint Paul and his attempt at legitimizing Christianity as a restoration of the pre-Jewish (or really, pre-legal) Abrahamic faith. Finally, with Chapter Five Azzam comes to the modern period—the death of God, the morality implicit in science, and the importance of modern art—then dedicating Chapter Six to the period of history Nietzsche projected beyond his own day, during which the meaning of God's death remained to be worked out.

The subject of each of these chapter is, of course, familiar to any serious reader of Nietzsche, all of them themes that are worked out across the whole trajectory of his writings. What marks out the uniqueness of Azzam's interpretation is the attention he pays to parallels between Nietzsche's genealogical analyses and those of (Nietzsche's) Paul. The chief point of interest here is the way that Azzam marks out a potential equivalence between Nietzsche's and Paul's respective attempts at *legitimizing* their radical breaks with history. Azzam's key point is nicely summarized in the following passage:

> Nietzsche's achievement lies, above all, in illuminating Dionysian art and paradisiacal science [that is, the science prohibited in the biblical story of the Fall] as that against which slave-morality reacts. On this basis, if the Antichrist remains dependent on its definition by Christianity as "anti-," it throws into oblivion the positive origin that Nietzsche's genealogy reveals, and thereafter remains bound to Christianity as its mere negative counterpart. . . . Alternatively, once the Antichrist assumes the original identities of art and science, the Antichrist dissolves its negativity. Here, Christ is remembered as anti-Dionysian, and therefore the Antichrist becomes the anti-anti-Dionysus: the Antichrist is the return of the unquestionably active Dionysus (49).

The point, here, is to recognize Nietzsche's self-designation as the Antichrist as active rather than reactive, and this depends on recognizing the whole history to which genealogical study attends as the history of reaction. "Christ" stands in for the reactive, and so the Antichrist labors in behalf of the active. All this, of course, relies on a certain attitude toward history. Azzam summarizes:

> History reveals before historical consciousness only those instincts that the historical narration points to as being part of history. . . . For the future is open for the realization of instincts of which we are not historically conscious (that is, instincts that at least were never realized in genealogically known history) (100).

For Azzam, Nietzsche's genealogy of Christian morality—stretching back into the historical conditions of its emergence and forward into its preservation in modernity's moral sensibility—reconstructs only the history of reaction, but it does so to reactivate what lies at the non-historical origins of that history: the Dionysian.

It is this that Azzam sees as running in parallel to Paul's structure of thought. For (Nietzsche's) Paul, the history of (law-bound) Judaism is a reactive history that obscures its non-historical origins: extra-legal Abrahamic faith. Just as Paul presents Christ as reactivating Abrahamic faith after the history of the law, Nietzsche presents the possibility of reactivating Dionysian tragic art after the history of (Pauline) Christianity. The two thinkers share a certain "logic of legitimization" (xvii), but where Paul is the first Christian Nietzsche is

119

emphatically the Antichrist. Naturally, along the way of staking out this argument, Azzam identifies other lesser points of potential parallel between Nietzsche and Paul. The most intriguing of them—and one worthy of notice here—is the possibility that Nietzsche's interpretation of the (largely one-sided) rivalry between Hegel and Schopenhauer repeats the relationship, in Paul's thought, between the *katechon* (the mysterious force that holds back the mystery of lawlessness) and the Antichrist. [1] This is rather suggestive, but Azzam unfortunately leaves the point largely underdeveloped, presenting it more as a provocation and a possibility than as a point of serious argument. Whether this point can be developed convincingly thus, unfortunately, remains to be seen.

The value of Azzam's book, however, lies less in occasional interpretive provocations than in its attempt at a reframing of the whole of Nietzsche's project as fundamentally driven by a Paul-like project of legitimization. Azzam attempts to reconstruct the whole trajectory of Nietzsche's genealogy, drawing from throughout Nietzsche's corpus, to reveal its Pauline and anti-Pauline motivations. For readers interested in understanding Nietzsche's interaction with Paul, this is invaluable. For readers already deeply familiar with Nietzsche, the argument is fascinating and worthy of critical attention. And for readers invested in some way in either Heidegger's or Deleuze's Nietzsche, the book serves to denaturalize a favored interpretation in the name of another systematic reading. Of these various readers the book might serve best, those it will serve least well are those interested in Nietzsche's approach to Paul without having yet become familiar with key Nietzschean ideas. Azzam assumes some facility with Nietzsche's writings and ideas, as well as some familiarity with points of contention in the secondary literature. It is thus better suited to reading by specialists interested in its interpretive thesis than to interested non-specialists, despite its obvious surface appeal to those who hope to gain from it a first familiarity with Nietzsche's critique of Paul and Pauline Christianity.

Despite what thus seems to me a minor failure in framing, Azzam's *Nietzsche Versus Paul* is an important—and daring—contribution. I hope it will receive serious attention and scrutiny. I especially hope that it will help to provoke more direct attempts to situate Nietzsche's Paul within the emergent conversation regarding the philosophical importance of Paul's thought

---

[1] The Pauline discussion of this point appears in 2 Thessalonians 2 in the New Testament. In the context of recent philosophical interpretation, this text has been the focus primarily of Giorgio Agamben's work. See Agamben.

Works Cited

Agamben, Giorgio. *The Time That Remains: A Commentary on the Letter to the Romans.* Translated by Patricia Dailey, Stanford University Press, 2005.

Badiou, Alain. *Saint Paul: The Foundation of Universalism.* Translated by Ray Brassier, Stanford University Press, 2003.

Salaquarda, Jörg. "Dionysus versus the Crucified One: Nietzsche's Understanding of the Apostle Paul." *Studies in Nietzsche and the Judaeo-Christian Tradition*, edited by James C. O'Flaherty, Timothy F. Sellner, and Robert M. Helm, University of North Caroline Press, 1985, pp. 100–29. Translated by Timothy F. Sellner.

Biographies of Contributors

Keith Ansell-Pearson holds a Personal Chair in Philosophy at the University of Warwick, a position he has held since 1998. He is the author and editor of books on Nietzsche, Bergson, and Deleuze, as well as the author of over eighty articles and review essays. He is currently researching a study of Nietzsche and Freud.

Daniel Conway is Professor of Philosophy and Humanities, and Affiliate Professor of Religious Studies and Film Studies, at Texas A&M University (USA). He lectures and publishes widely on topics in post-Kantian European philosophy, political theory, religion, literature, and film.

Matthew Dennis is writing his thesis on philosophical self-cultivation on the Joint Ph.D. programme at the universities of Monash (Australia) and Warwick (UK). He works on in ethics and aesthetics in the modern European philosophical tradition, Hellenistic philosophy, and contemporary virtue theory. He is currently completing two articles on contemporary virtue ethical readings of Nietzsche to be published in 2017.

Jennifer Gammage is a Ph.D. student and teaching fellow at DePaul University where she also works as an instructor for the Arnold L. Mitchem Fellows Program. Her interests unfold from the intersection of hermeneutics, philosophy of history, temporality, psychoanalysis, and the event of revolution.

Peter S. Groff is Associate Professor at Bucknell University. He has written on Nietzsche, Islamic philosophy, and comparative issues across philosophical traditions. His most recent scholarship focuses on establishing a dialogue of sorts between Nietzsche and select classical Islamic philosophers, by way of their creative appropriation of certain Greek and Hellenistic themes.

Jill Marsden is a senior lecturer in the School of the Arts at the University of Bolton. She is the author of *After Nietzsche: Notes Towards a Philosophy of Ecstasy* (Palgrave 2002) and a range of articles on continental philosophy and literature.

Joseph M. Spencer received a Ph.D. in philosophy from the University of New Mexico and is now Visiting Assistant Professor in the College of Religious Education at Brigham Young University. He is the author of several books and numerous articles focused on philosophy and theology. He serves as the associate director of the Mormon Theology Seminar, and is an associate editor of the *Journal of Book of Mormon Studies*.

Federico Testa is a Philosophy Ph.D. candidate at Monash University (Australia) and at the University of Warwick (England). His research explores the notions of life, normativity and vitalism in the works of Michel Foucault and Georges Canguilhem. He is translating Guyau's *La morale d'Épicure*. His principal areas of interest are contemporary French philosophy, history of philosophy, aesthetics and political theory. He holds a Master's degree in Philosophy and a Master's degree in History and Theory of Art, and he has taught in universities in Brazil and Australia.

Willow Verkerk is a Lecturer in Philosophy at the Centre for Research in Modern European Philosophy at Kingston University, London. She specializes in 19th and 20th century German and French Philosophy and Feminist Philosophy. Her work has appeared in *Journal of Nietzsche Studies*, *Philosophy and Literature*, *Philosophy Now*, *Symposium: Canadian Journal for Continental Philosophy*, and will appear in *The Spell of Capital: Reification and Spectacle* (University of Amsterdam Press), and *philoSOPHIA: A Journal of Continental Feminism*.

Submission Guidelines

To be considered for publication in *The Agonist* we require:

- A page with your full name, your academic affiliation (if applicable), address, email, and phone number.
- A short summary (200-300 words) sent together with your work, indicating the topic of your submission.
- A 250-word bio, the length of your manuscript/submission, and a short list of prior publications.

Please use biographical listings of current contributors as models.

Essays should be between 3,000 and 5,000 words.

Contributors are expected to check all typographical issues, such as italicizing the titles of works of art, in the Word file. If there are issues regarding the appropriateness of the text, those matters will be discussed with the contributor. If there are proofing issues, the contributor will be notified to make the corrections. Submitted texts will not be altered by us. *The Agonist* does not return submitted manuscripts, accept unsolicited manuscripts, or consider manuscripts that are under review elsewhere or that have been previously published.

BOOK REVIEWS:
The Agonist accepts review copies of books on or related to Nietzsche (see About) and will seek reviewers to write on them. Book publishers interested in forwarding review copies can contact the editors at nceditors@nietzschecircle.com or you can use our contact form. Please submit initially a proposal for an essay, which must be original work by the submitting author. For further details, please see Submission Guidelines below.
Any work received that does not follow the appropriate guidelines will not be read. If you have any questions with regard to our guidelines or submission policy, please contact us

HOW TO SUBMIT:
The abstract (300 words maximum) and the submission should be sent to: nceditors@nietzschecircle.com. Once approved by the *The Agonist* Editorial Board, a deadline will be determined for the submission. The response time may

vary from 2-5 weeks, so please be patient.

SPECIFIC GUIDELINES:
1. *The Agonist* uses the *MLA style* (see www.mla.org).

2. All submissions must be submitted as a double-spaced Word-document, using a point twelve TNR (12) font with 1" margins on all sides. For footnotes, please use point ten (10) font.

3. The paragraphs must be separated from each other; indent 5 spaces in the beginning of each paragraph.

4. Quotations that exceed three lines must be indented and separated from the body of the text into its own paragraph. The lengthy citations are also single-spaced, as are the footnotes.

5. Please note that page numbers go into the upper right hand corner with your last name.

6. Italics are to be used for author's *emphases*, book and journal titles, and foreign terms.

7. Quotations from Nietzsche's works should be followed in the main text by parenthetical references to the work in abbreviation followed by section or note numbers: e.g., (BT §7), (GS §124), (GM III §7), (TI "Ancients" §3). For a complete list of standard abbreviations, see below. The translation being cited should be indicated in a footnote to the first quotation from the work. If the author is rendering Nietzsche's German into English, each quotation should be footnoted with a reference to a standard critical German edition of Nietzsche's works, preferably the KSA. All other scholarly references should be given in the footnotes.

8. In the case of essays on visual art, images and captions should be embedded in the text. Images and caption texts must be submitted both separately (on a separate cover sheet) and as the Word file in order to be prepared for publication.

9. In the case of essays on visual art, it is necessary for the contributor to obtain images and caption texts. Generally, these are available from galleries and museum press or public relations offices, along with the needed permissions.

10. Images must be at least 300 dpi, at a print scale sufficient to fit properly in a normal-sized PDF file. (8 1/2 by 11 inches—please see current The Agonist PDF files for examples of the scale.)

11. *The Agonist* does not offer compensation to contributors.

12. Copyright for all published texts will be held jointly by the contributor and *The Agonist*.

13. Manuscript submissions and all related materials and other correspondence should be sent to: nceditors(at)nietzschecircle.com.

14. Books for review and all inquiries concerning books listed as received for review should be directed to the book editors.

STANDARD ABBREVIATIONS:

As noted above, references to Nietzsche's writings are to be included in the body of the essay using the standard English title abbreviations indicated below. With reference to translations, Roman numerals denote a standard subdivision within a single work in which the sections are not numbered consecutively (e.g., On the Genealogy of Morals), Arabic numerals denote the section number rather than the page number, and "P" denotes Nietzsche's Prefaces.

Unless the author is translating, the published translation used should be indicated with a footnote to the initial citation reference.

References to the editions by Giorgio Colli and Mazzino Montinari take the following forms:

Kritische Gesamtausgabe (KGW) (Berlin: de Gruyter, 1967—) is cited by division number (Roman), followed by volume number (Arabic), followed by the fragment number.

Kritische Studienausgabe (KSA) (Berlin: de Gruyter, 1980) is cited by volume number (Arabic) followed by the fragment number.

Briefwechsel: Kritische Gesamtausgabe (KGB) (Berlin: de Gruyter, 1975—) is cited by division number (Roman), followed by volume number (Arabic), followed by page number.

Sämtliche Briefe: Kritische Studienausgabe (KSB) (Berlin: de Gruyter, 1986) is cited by volume number (Arabic) followed by page number.

References to *Thus Spoke Zarathustra* list the part number and chapter title, e.g., (Z: 4 "On Science").
References to *Twilight of the Idols* and *Ecce Homo* list abbreviated chapter title and section number, e.g., (TI "Ancients" §3) or (EH "Books" BGE §2).

References to works in which sections are too long to be cited helpfully by section number should cite section number then page number, e.g., (SE §3, p. 142), with the translation/edition footnoted.

A = *The Antichrist*
AOM = *Assorted Opinions and Maxims*
BGE = *Beyond Good and Evil*
BT = *The Birth of Tragedy*
CW = *The Case of Wagner*
D = *Daybreak / Dawn*
DS = *David Strauss, the Writer and the Confessor*
EH = *Ecce Homo* ["Wise," "Clever," "Books," "Destiny"]
FEI = "On the Future of our Educational Institutions"
GM = *On the Genealogy of Morals*
GOA = *Nietzsches Werke* (Grossoktavausgabe)
GS = *The Gay Science / Joyful Wisdom*
HS = "Homer's Contest"
HCP = "Homer and Classical Philology"
HH = *Human, All Too Human*
HL = *On the Use and Disadvantage of History for Life*
KGB = *Briefwechsel: Kritische Gesamtausgabe*
KGW = *Kritische Gesamtausgabe*
KSA = *Kritische Studienausgabe*
KSB = *Sämtliche Briefe: Kritische Studienausgabe*
LR = "Lectures on Rhetoric"
MA = *Nietzsches Gesammelte Werke* (Musarionausgabe)
NCW = *Nietzsche contra Wagner*
PPP = *Pre-Platonic Philosophers*
PTA = *Philosophy in the Tragic Age of the Greeks*
RWB = *Richard Wagner in Bayreuth*
SE = *Schopenhauer as Educator*
TI = *Twilight of the Idols* ["Maxims," "Socrates," "Reason," "World," "Morality," "Errors," "Improvers," "Germans," "Skirmishes," "Ancients," "Hammer"] TL

= "On Truth and Lies in an Extra-moral Sense"
UM = *Untimely Meditations / Thoughts Out of Season*
WDB = *Werke in drei Bänden* (Ed. Karl Schlechta)
WP = *The Will to Power*
WPh = "We Philologists"
WS = *The Wanderer and his Shadow*
WLN = *Writings from the Late Notebooks*
Z = *Thus Spoke Zarathustra*